# THE CREATIVE ART OF
# GARDEN DESIGN

The garden at Greenways, Walmer, Kent, designed by Percy Cane. (Photograph by Country Life)

# THE CREATIVE ART OF

# GARDEN DESIGN

## PERCY CANE

COUNTRY LIFE LIMITED LONDON

*First published in 1967 by*
*Country Life Limited*
*Tower House, Southampton Street, WC2*
*Printed in Great Britain by*
*The Camelot Press Limited*
*London and Southampton*

© Percy Cane 1966

# Contents

INTRODUCTION     11

1 FLOWERING PLANTS AND HERBACEOUS BORDERS     25

2 ROSE GARDENS     32

3 WATER GARDENS     41

4 GLADES     48

5 JAPANESE GARDENS     59

6 ASPECTS OF DESIGN     65

7 GARDEN PLANS     102

INDEX     119

# Illustrations

## PHOTOGRAPHS

|  |  |  |
|---|---|---|
|  | The garden at Greenways, Walmer, Kent | *frontispiece* |
| 1 | Knole, Sevenoaks, Kent | *following page* 16 |
| 2 | Penshurst Place, Kent | 16 |
| 3 | Paved court at Hoare's Bank, Fleet Street | 16 |
| 4 | The White House, Highgate, London | 16 |
| 5 | Terraces at Hascombe Court, Surrey | 32 |
| 6 | Herbaceous borders, Bowhill, Chichester | 32 |
| 7 | Rose garden at Busbridge Wood, Surrey | 32 |
| 8 | A formal rose garden, Westfields, Bedfordshire | 40 |
| 9 | Terracing at Monteviot, Scotland | 40 |
| 10 | Rose garden at Ridge End, Worcestershire | 40 |
| 11 | Formal garden at Hillside, Warwickshire | 40 |
| 12 | Pergola at Boden's Ride, Ascot | 40 |
| 13 | A formal pool at Hascombe Court | 52 |
| 14 | A pool in the glade at Westwoods, Surrey | 52 |
| 15 | Stream garden at Westfields, Bedfordshire | 52 |
| 16 | Formal pool at Westfields | 56 |
| 17 | A garden glade in Buckinghamshire | 56 |
| 18 | A rhododendron glade at Busbridge Wood | 56 |
| 19 | Garden glade at Westfields | 56 |
| 20 | A woodland glade | 60 |
| 21 | Garden of Tenryuji Temple, Kyoto | 60 |

| | | |
|---|---|---|
| 22 | Garden of Katsura Villa, Kyoto | 60 |
| 23 | The lake at The Aviary, Southall | 64 |
| 24 | The lake side glade at The Aviary | 64 |
| 25 | Terrace at Ardleigh, Chigwell | 64 |
| 26 | Formal garden at Frognal, Hampstead | 64 |
| 27 | Old Hall Cottage, Frinton-on-Sea, Essex | 64 |
| 28 | The Cottage, Le Touquet | 64 |
| 29 | Informal lawn at Woodford, Essex | 72 |
| 30 | Curving steps, Woodford | 72 |
| 31 | Lily pool at The White House, Sandwich, Kent | 72 |
| 32 | The sunken garden at The White House, Sandwich | 72 |
| 33 | Lily pool and oak tree at Hungerdown, Wiltshire | 72 |
| 34 | The glade at Hungerdown | 72 |
| 35 | Terracing at Hungerdown | 72 |
| 36 | Formal garden, Hungerdown | 72 |
| 37 | Hillside; the formal pool | 72 |
| 38 | The main lawn, Hillside | 72 |
| 39 | Herbaceous borders at Langham Hall, Essex | 72 |
| 40 | The rotunda at Stonely Woods, Yorkshire | 72 |
| 41 | Borders in the paved garden at Stonely Woods | 80 |
| 42 | The walled garden at The Vern, Herefordshire | 80 |
| 43 | The Mill House, Fittleworth, Sussex | 80 |
| 44 | Terrace at The Mill House, Fittleworth | 80 |
| 45 | Pilgrim's Cottage, Itchenor, Sussex | 80 |
| 46 | Courtyard at Pilgrim's Cottage | 80 |
| 47 | Herbaceous borders at Hascombe Court | 80 |
| 48 | A villa on the French Riviera | 80 |

49  Hascombe Court, the paved terrace                    80

50  The steeply sloping garden at Westwoods               88

51  Formal water garden at Westfields                     88

52  Informal water garden at Westfields                   88

53  The great staircase, Dartington Hall, Devon           88

54  Woodland glade at Dartington Hall                     88

55  View from the highest terrace, Dartington Hall        88

56  Formal garden at Monteviot, Scotland                  88

57  River garden, Monteviot                               88

58  Glade at Chestham Park, Sussex                        88

59  Formal walk at Chestham Park                          88

60  The East Walk, Chestham Park                          96

61  Walled garden at Milton, Peterborough                 96

62  Lower gardens at Falkland Palace, Fife                96

63  Cypress walk, Lower Sandhill, Sussex                  96

64  Terrace at Lower Sandhill                             96

65  Cloisters at Llannerch Park                           96

66  Formal pool at Llannerch Park                         96

## PLANS AND DRAWINGS

A colonnaded and paved court                        *page* 16

Reconstruction of gardens at Hungerdown, Wiltshire       20

Combination and contrast of gardens                      22

Design for new formal gardens at Woburn Abbey            24

Herbaceous borders                                       29

Shrub border                                             29

| | |
|---|---|
| Rose gardens | 33, 34, 35, 37 |
| A villa on the French Riviera | 101 |
| A lakeland garden | 103 |
| A small town garden | 104 |
| A rectangular garden | 105 |
| A tiny garden | 106 |
| Elaborate treatment of a small garden | 107 |
| A herb garden | 108 |
| A garden on chalk | 109 |
| Simple formality | 110 |
| Easy to maintain | 111 |
| Connecting separate gardens | 112 |
| An octagonal garden | 113 |
| An illusion of space | 114 |
| A suburban garden | 115 |
| A bungalow garden | 116 |
| A formal garden | 117 |
| A feeling of spaciousness | 118 |

## ACKNOWLEDGMENTS

The author desires to express his thanks to the owners of the gardens illustrated in this book, who have kindly allowed him to use photographs and plans of their gardens.

Grateful acknowledgment is also made to Sir Charles Richmond Brown, who provided the photographs of Stoneley Woods, to Mr James N. Campbell, Mr Chaplin Jones and Messrs R. W. Luckins Ltd., who took most of the remaining photographs, to Mr Harold White, who drew most of the sketches, and to A. and Isa Macrae-Taylor for their generous help in reading the draft text.

# Introduction

DESIGNING GARDENS is an art, but as in painting, the man who knows little about art but knows what he likes, enjoys a picture that observes certain basic principles. As in all the arts there are periods of growth and of changing fashion, but the principles remain constant. To make a beautiful garden the garden maker must know not only what he is doing, but also why he is doing it. And to make the complete unity of design so necessary if the results are to be good, the garden maker must have a knowledge of the technique of garden design, and of gardening and arboriculture.

He must have a plan like the studies an artist draws, before he begins, for a garden is a picture that every year paints through the seasons, changing with the years as plants grow tall, but its main lines—its trees and larger shrubs—must stay and its success depends on how well they are grouped in the picture. If he starts in a haphazard way without a plan, the different parts that together make the whole garden will almost certainly be out of proportion and badly related. I hope in the following chapters to show how a successful garden may be achieved. And by a successful garden I mean a garden that gives in its proportions, in the relation of the different parts that together make up the whole, and by the loveliness of its colour harmonies, a keen and lively sense of pleasure to the beholder.

Therefore we have to think of the garden as a complete entity, which we can walk round —something akin to a picture gallery, only a picture gallery that is alive and growing. In a small garden, perhaps no larger than a Chelsea Flower Show garden, we can have a single picture, but seen from, say, the windows, the entrance and from the panoramic view we obtain when walking round it. We cannot, however, mix two pictures, two styles, blending, for instance, Constable's 'Hay Wain' with a Dutch interior by Rembrandt, or it will look a mess. In a larger garden we can have a succession of pictures, the divisions being their frames, or we can flow them from one to another by means of centre vistas carried through the different gardens. If this planning is done skilfully it will result in an effect of greater space; if done badly we can make a fairly large garden look tiny and shut in.

## Definition of boundaries

Local conditions will affect the design of any garden in a considerable degree but a few general principles may be of assistance. To mark the boundaries of the property, quickthorn, which makes an impenetrable hedge, always looks well in the country. Holly, too, is excellent but is expensive to buy and grows very slowly. Alternatively, for more extensive sites, belts of trees, coniferous or deciduous or both, could be planted to enclose the whole or part of the property. Such trees should be planted as protection from the colder quarters.

The forecourt or entrance front should have its own quiet dignity, a dignity in its own way as satisfying as the greater luxuriance of the gardens for which, by its contrast, it is the nicest preparation.

A terrace, larger or smaller to suit the size and character of the residence, will be the connecting link between house and garden. The terrace will be formal. It may be higher than, or it may be level with the lawn on to which it opens. To create a feeling of comparative spaciousness the lawn should be clear of trees near the house, but farther away trees or groups of trees and shrubs, skilfully placed, can be made to give an illusion of greater distance than actually exists.

*Contrast of design*

In any but the smallest gardens there should be contrast, both of form and of planting between adjoining gardens, that is, an empty lawn garden should lead to a more elaborately planted garden—a rose garden, an iris garden, or perhaps a lavender garden. The nature of the planting would not matter so long as it is a full garden. An effective contrast could be created by making an alley or walk of turf between two gardens of colour. This law of contrast is dealt with more fully in the description of a garden on page 22.

The gardens of Great Britain show in a very marked degree the influence of the design of other countries and of earlier times. Partly owing to climate, and in part to the inborn creative artistry of the Italian people, there came at the time of the Renaissance an exuberance of inventive design that has never been surpassed, and the formal gardens of Italy with their statuary and ornament have influenced numbers of British gardens.

The classic gardens of France, too, are generally dignified and show an excellent sense of proportion, but they depend more for their character on the formal use of trees than on flowering plants. Versailles, with its great formal pools and its architectural features, is an outstanding example. Possibly the garden, with its extensive vistas, is rather beyond human scale but others of the French chateaux, Saint Cloud, Rambouillet and Fontainebleau, are examples of French design at its finest. Although so much attention is not given to flowers, parterres of flowers in set patterns enter into the design of many French gardens. This broderie can be seen in Paris as part of the setting for the Louvre as well as in many of the finer French gardens.

In spite of its vagaries, the climate of Great Britain encourages this inherent love of gardens and gardening, for it is doubtful if there is in any other country a greater variety of trees, shrubs and plants at the garden maker's service. But this very love of gardens, because it is, so far as design is concerned, often untrained, is the cause of so many gardens falling short of the highest standards. The classic gardens of this country evidence a very high quality of design and they are, as a rule, so right in their general character with the architecture of the houses for which they form the setting. For examples of these see Plates 1 and 2 of Knole and Penshurst facing page 16.

## Influence of climate

In improving the quality of design in our gardens we should take into consideration climatic conditions and, while profiting to the full from the design of other countries, still keep our national character and tradition, for our tradition is long and good. Because of the climate here, which is on the whole favourable to growing good turf, we in this country can have lawns, an immense asset. Without good turf it is impossible to have extensive lawns, only comparatively narrow alleys or walks, and those of gravel or some similar material.

## Formal design

The term formal applied to gardens is of the widest application and to define it exactly is almost impossible. Probably the nearest definition would be to say that any formal garden must consist in its design of straight lines or of geometrical curves. As examples, formal rose or flower gardens could be square, rectangular, octagonal or indeed they could be of any shape, or they could be a combination of any shapes that did not include curving lines other than geometrical curves. There is, however, a dignity in straight lines just as curving lines rightly used can give us some of the loveliest of garden scenes. Terraces must as a rule be formal. Herbaceous walks or borders are generally better straight although this is not always the case. But it really comes back to the fact that any garden should, so to speak, grow out of the site on which it is being made.

The formality of formal gardens can be much increased by the symmetrical placing of certain types of cypress and juniper. *Chamaecyparis lawsoniana allumii* or *Juniperus chinensis* with their columnar habit of growth are very suitable for this purpose, but the colour of *J. chinensis*, a rather brownish-green, is not so pleasing as the attractive grey-green of *C. l. allumii*. The golden form of *J. chinensis, J. c. aurea*, too, is equally good for its close columnar shape but not for its colour, a slightly rusty gold, and colours near it should be chosen with care. Almost any shade of yellow, bronze, brown or gold would, however, tone with it happily. Scarlet could be used to heighten colour values, blues would be permissible, but they should be clear blues, not mauves, which generally have some shade of pink in them. With *C. l. allumii*, so pleasingly grey-green, any range of colours may be used and, an additional advantage, the colour scheme can, if bedding plants or annuals are used, be changed from year to year. With the junipers, good as their form is, this is not so. Their colour limits the choice of colours to be used near them.

## Symmetry in planting

The term symmetry perhaps needs some definition. It may be described as the placing of any taller or outstanding trees exactly opposite, and probably at regular distances. These trees should be generally of the cupressus type. Other trees in this category are *Juniperus hibernica*, the Irish juniper, clipped green or golden yews, clipped box and *Chamaecyparis lawsoniana fletcheri*. This has lovely grey-green foliage, soft and feathery in texture and it seldom grows more than 10 feet high, a distinct advantage in small gardens. The symmetrical placing of suitable trees or shrubs can, too, be used to heighten immensely the effect of, say, a walk between hedges of green yew. Of the golden yews, *Taxus baccata standishii* is the best variety for the purpose, and planted symmetrically in pairs down the length of a grass walk between green hedges, it would be distinctive. The green hedges, against which the golden yews would stand in sharp relief, would show how rich greens and golds in their varying shades can be. As *T. b. standishii* grows very slowly, only about $1\frac{1}{2}$ or 2 inches a year, it would be advisable to plant fairly large specimens. Alternatively *T. b. fastigiata aurea*, which is not so slow growing, could be planted. With countless drops of dew sparkling in early sunlight such a walk could be very lovely. For a wider walk cypresses could be used. They should be spaced at greater distances, say at 25 feet or more apart, and they could be planted in front of hedges of the same variety of cypress or yew. When cypresses are used the walk must be wider, say 20 feet or more, to allow for their greater size when fully grown.

## Aesthetic value of green

The colour values of green in its many shades are seldom fully recognised. A square, circular or octagonal garden carpeted with lawn with no flowers, but relying for its interest on a stone sundial or other suitable ornament would be an unusual contrast to gardens of flowers. To make use of Italian influence, stone or wooden seats or benches placed back against the hedges, with perhaps a stone or marble fountain basin in the centre, would be decoration enough. As an interlude between flower gardens such a garden would not only be distinctive but it would, by its contrast, very much increase the colour values of the flower gardens. And it would require very little upkeep, only mowing, and trimming the hedges twice a year. The flowers of nymphaeas are so lovely that they could be grown in the pool with no other flowers to compete with them.

The formality of hedges is in its own way a valuable asset in designing or making a garden. Hedges are like green walls and they can be planned to extend the architectural lines of the house into the gardens forming, as it were, an extension to it of living green. Hedges, too, can soften boundaries. A brick wall enclosing a garden limits its apparent size, whereas a green hedge merges into its surroundings in an easy way so that it could be difficult to tell where the garden ends.

## Courts

A courtyard is defined by the Oxford dictionary as a space enclosed by walls or buildings. Courts may be small or large—size does not matter. They may be enriched with ornaments, not too many but showing real merit in their design and craftsmanship. Planting may be confined to climbing plants on the walls; there may be beds of shrubs or plants, or plants may be grown in pots or tubs, the latter chosen to form a decoration in themselves.

There are many small town gardens that might aptly be described as back yards, with all the implications that such a description implies. Such spaces are often enclosed by buildings or walls and it might seem difficult to make them attractive. Space in London and other cities is, however, aesthetically as well as financially valuable and such yards can with a little ingenuity and work often be transformed into delightful courts (Plate 3). In Rome, Florence and in other Italian cities there are courtyards, with a fountain in the centre and with creeper covered walls; sometimes there is a tree, with its grateful shade, so welcome in hot climates. In this country, on the other hand, light and sunshine are welcome and given these attributes an unattractive yard can be transformed into a delightful court. If small it should be paved as paving will have the effect of making it seem larger and is much easier to keep clean and in good order than turf, which, in a confined space will probably become bare and in wet weather muddy. Topiary, too, could be introduced. The clear-cut shapes of yew or box, placed where accent is needed, can be used to enrich many small courts.

At The White House, Highgate (Plate 4), there is a court on to which a big window of a music studio opens. The court is paved and enclosed on all sides by walls, which are greyish-white, an excellent colour as a background for flowers and foliage. It is decorated with stone urns, a stone bench and a carved stone panel in bas-relief let into the wall over the bench. The light foliage of silver birches in tubs, an effective but unusual way of growing them in a confined space, is charming against the white walls, and zonal pelargoniums give splashes of vivid colour. The architectural effect is enhanced by wrought iron railing on the parapet of one of the walls. But the railing, apparently a safeguard, is decorative rather than useful, for as one cannot get to the top of the wall one cannot fall from it, but it does support the long stems of a *Wisteria sinensis*.

A garden on a higher level may give the opportunity of changing a terrace into a patio or formal court. An outstanding example of a court of real distinction is in Carl Milles's

A paved court with colonnading and a stone shelter

garden in Stockholm. Mr Milles is a sculptor with a world-wide reputation and his garden, or rather the part of which I am writing, is a sculptor's garden. In it there are few plants but the sculptural effect is enhanced by the placing of close-growing columnar cypress, echoes, as it were, of the classical stone columns supporting the beams that complete the enclosure of the court. The spaces between the columns are like large open windows overlooking the lower gardens.

1. The classic gardens at Knole, Kent

2. Penshurst, Kent; formal parterres and pool

3. A paved court with stone benches, and urns filled with bedding plants and small trees at Hoare's Bank, Fleet Street

4. The White House, Highgate; paved court furnished with a stone bench, a stone bas-relief panel and plants in tubs

To emphasise height is to add to the dramatic effect of any garden. As an illustration of this the use of columns crowning some height would be finer in appearance than would the same columns in a valley or even on level ground. This can be seen in some foreign cities built on hilly sites. In Rome, for instance, columns and balustrading guarding some garden or terrace high above the lower levels gain immensely in dramatic quality from the height. But in this country it is more usual to have patios or courts on level ground or perhaps one storey above ground level. The sketch on page 16 is for a paved garden levelled out of a slope on a hillside. Standing well above the lower garden the colonnade and entablature show clearly against the sky. Framed by the coupled columns there is an entrance to a rose garden at the far end. The steps in the right hand corner lead to a walk on a higher level while the stone shelter in the left hand corner overlooks extensive views.

At the villa illustrated in Plate 48, high above the drive, there was ground, a long rectangle, on to which principal rooms opened. This ground was bounded on the north by low stone walls which supported a steeply rising bank. On the southern side the wall rising from the drive was built high enough to form a parapet. Paved, with a carved stone fountain, masses of richly coloured flowers growing over the low walls and vines and roses draping the columns, this ground would become a very attractive court. The colonnading rising from the low southern wall with seats and some stone flower troughs would furnish and give it distinction. Light and shade are stronger in southern sunlight than in more northern climates and the contrast of horizontal and vertical lines is heightened by the tall cypresses and the shadows they cast.

In such courts there is much to be said in favour of having plants such as pelargoniums and fuchsias, of which there are a number of charming varieties, in stone vases or troughs. The vases or troughs should be a decoration in themselves and the plants can be changed from time to time, a decided advantage in an enclosed space. Some clipped bays, box or green or golden yews should be included for the contrast of their evergreen foliage with the flowering plants and because they will help to furnish the court in winter. Tulips and narcissi can fill the boxes in early spring and an unusual effect may be obtained in summer by planting a low Japanese maple, *Acer palmatum dissectum atropurpureum*, in each tub or box, with the deep pink geranium Charles Turner under the maple. The colour of this geranium tones beautifully with the crimson leaves of the maples.

## Small gardens

To consider small gardens first, the character of the house will necessarily influence their design. In small gardens the boundaries may be walls, they may be hedges. It does not matter which, but the nature of the boundaries will affect the design to a considerable degree. As an instance, in a small paved court the interest and colour of plants would be given by roses and other climbing plants on the walls. Plants, too, could be grown in tubs or in lead or stone urns which would in themselves form an effective decoration, and a seat or seats could be an integral part of the design. In such a court there could well be one or more objects of interest but one such object should, like the fireplace in a room, be outstanding, a focal point to which any others are secondary.

## Medium-sized gardens

There is a technique of design for medium-sized gardens, a knowledge of which will be of material assistance to the amateur gardener. Gardens within this range will consist of two or more parts and in them there must be contrast of design and there must, too, be contrast in the character of the planting. To achieve contrast of design, an approximately square or a rectangular garden could lead into a circular or an octagonal garden. The first garden should be what I will call an open garden, that is, its centre space could be lawn unbroken by any beds, but probably surrounded by borders, while in the second, the whole or the greater part of the centre space could be utilised as a formal pattern of beds, a mass of colour, so much the more effective seen across the plain green lawn.

To illustrate these points the plan on page 105 starting from the house shows first of all a paved terrace and a lawn with its paved surround, an open garden. The second part is separated from the first by a wall which sweeps down from the higher outer walls to a lower level across the garden. In this second space the panel of rose beds is set in turf on three sides and on the fourth it borders the wide paved walk which extends for the length of the garden. To note again the points of contrasting interest, first there is the open garden of paving and lawn; next to it there is the rose garden, set in paving, its surrounding borders planted with shrubs and flowering plants, the colours of which would be chosen to harmonise with and throw into higher relief the colours of the roses. The third and last garden is again a contrast. In it, at the end of the long paved walk, there is a pool (A). This garden, its borders filled with vivid colour, scarlet, orange, purple, etc., with its open centre lawn, and with the lily pool and fountain as its chief interest, would be again entirely different from either of the other two. Interest would be reawakened by the pool at the far end of the garden.

A pool in shadow can be a depressing sight and if a fountain or pool is the central object the water must be in sunlight. Alternatively, an Italian wellhead could, in a suitable setting, constitute the centre piece round which the garden is created. Individual taste, however, would decide what would be suitable. And in this would lie much of the interest of making such a garden. When large enough and open enough the garden could be finer and the formality of the design increased if stone flags were laid to a width of from 3 to 4 feet between the flower borders and a central lawn.

It is really in gardens of two or more divisions that scope for design begins, and, still considering gardens of medium size, it should be easily possible to divide them into two or more parts. A further point in design is that if even a comparatively small garden can be planned so that it is possible to walk round it, it will seem both larger and decidedly more interesting than if this were not possible. The connecting way could be a turf walk with flower borders on either side, or alternatively the connecting way could be planted as a glade of flowering trees and shrubs, only it would need greater width in which to make it.

## Larger gardens

These should, so to speak, grow out of the site on which they are to be made, but this statement calls for elucidation. As a general rule it is advisable to work in harmony with the atmosphere or character of the site rather than to go contrary to it. As an instance, a level site offers wonderful opportunities for making gardens appear so much more extensive than would be the case if the levels were broken by artificial hills and valleys. No, there is nothing to be afraid of in levels any more than there is in a sloping or hilly site. Level sites need to be diversified by skilfully placed specimen trees or groups of trees and shrubs, while on hilly sites the task is the more difficult one of making enough level lawns or walks, without which any garden would create a restless feeling. But on hilly or sloping sites terraces and steps will be necessary and, skilfully treated, can be most effective.

In more extensive grounds the garden as a whole will consist of several gardens, each with its individual character and each happily related to the adjoining gardens. The treatment of these separate parts would depend very much on the character of the site. There might be a rose garden, a herbaceous walk, a formal flower garden, or a garden of scented shrubs and flowers. There could be borders or gardens in separate colours and, if space allows, a glade of flowering trees and shrubs. Glades or borders of trees and shrubs are labour-saving as, other than pruning, they need little attention. And there might be a rock garden, although a garden that is slightly Japanese in character could be altogether more beautiful than what is generally known as a rock garden. Such a garden would need very much less stone and fewer plants than a rock garden.

Having named the various gardens which together make a larger garden, say from one acre in extent, let us consider how such individual gardens should be best arranged. Here there is so much latitude that it is practically impossible to lay down rules, but a few general principles may help. As in smaller gardens the house—the main garden front— should, in most cases, open first on to a paved terrace and thence on to a lawn on which, if extensive enough, specimen trees growing in the turf would give a feeling of age and maturity. For this reason any existing trees that are suitably placed should be retained.

A fault common with amateurs, and sometimes with professionals, when planting young

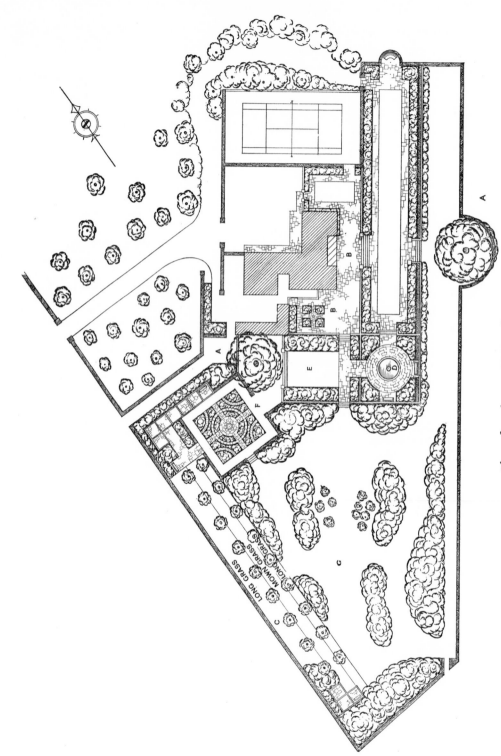

Plan of gardens at Hungerdown

trees, is to plant them too close together. In this connection it is good practice to stake on the ground not only the exact position of the tree trunks but also the ultimate spread of their branches. Although trees only attain their full character with age they are attractive while they are growing. They can also be encouraged to grow by feeding and good cultivation. It will help trees to grow more quickly, too, if, to provide shelter and to draw them up, a few silver birches are planted round each tree, the birches to be transplanted or cut down as the permanent trees grow.

*Diverse interests*

But to return to the arrangement of those parts that are more particularly gardens, there should be diversity of interest in the relation of one garden to another. It is difficult to state how this should be done because any existing features of merit should be retained. As an instance the two very fine oaks (lettered A in the plan shown on page 20) at Hungerdown dominate the gardens and had not only to be retained but the design had to be made subservient to them. For a more detailed description of this garden, see page 71.

To illustrate my points as to the contrast and arrangement of gardens more clearly the plan on page 22 shows the main garden front of the house opening on to a paved terrace. From this terrace proportionally wide steps go down to a lawn (A). This lawn follows the general lines of the garden. In it there are wide flower borders close to the hedges and these, with the flagged paths, make it a formal flower garden. From here more steps descend to a walk (C), the borders of which are planted chiefly with shrubs. This walk, compared with the first spacious lawn, is narrow. This treatment gives a double contrast, the change from the wide upper lawn to the long narrow walk and the change from the perennial flower-filled borders in the first, upper garden to the borders planted with shrubs in the long narrow walk. From the long walk more wide steps descend to another formal garden (D) at the lowest level. Here again is contrast of design, for whereas the upper garden had an empty lawn, surrounded by flower borders and paved paths, this lowest garden has as its central feature a formal lily pool (E). From the pool garden, one ascends to an outer glade which encircles the formal gardens (F). This glade, curving into a wide lawn, is planted almost entirely with shrubs and shrub roses and furnishes yet another contrast both in its design and in its planting. To emphasise the contrast even more, the upper flower-bordered lawn and the pool garden are at their best during summer and autumn while the long narrow shrub walk and the outer glade borders, at their best in spring and early summer, are later green interludes which, just because they are principally green, heighten considerably the colour values of the flower gardens.

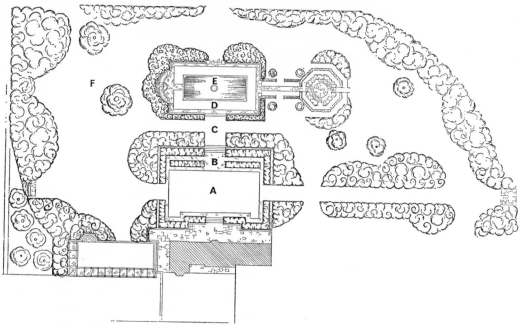

Plan showing contrast and arrangement of gardens within the main garden

## Contrast between formal and informal design

Situated more or less centrally in its 3,000 acres of richly timbered parkland, Woburn Abbey, the seat of the Duke and Duchess of Bedford, is an imposing pile of buildings standing in isolated magnificence. The Abbey is surrounded by 40 acres of pleasure grounds —a park in itself. The pleasure grounds and, I believe, the park were laid out originally to designs by Humphry Repton; at the present time Repton's work is most noticeable from the main entrance front. It is interesting to the connoisseur of garden design in this country, standing on the steps, to notice Repton's work. Looking along the main drive, which carries one's eye to the broad stretch of water in the middle distance, one can see how orderly his planning has been—the broad sweeps of level turf which throw into higher relief the bold masses of trees, chiefly hardwoods, giving way to gradually rising turf, a smooth green carpet framed by massive woods on either side, disappearing over the rise into illimitable distance.

Repton's planning is again discernible in long rides in the pleasure grounds. The cedar avenue, extending from the great *Cedrus libanii* in the centre of the main courtyard to a stone temple of classic design which terminates it on the boundary of the pleasure grounds, is a part of the gardens entirely suited in its proportions and the grandeur of its conception to the stately architecture of the Abbey.

There are, too, the remains of an araucaria avenue, with here and there a fine tree still standing, enough to show its original extent. This avenue must have been striking when its trees were at their best but it is doubtful if it fitted into the garden scenery as happily as did the cedars. Both cedar and araucaria avenues are, however, interesting as showing the greater use that was formerly made of trees in the design of extensive country estates.

Over the years the pleasure grounds have lost much of their original character. In them there are many very fine cedars, oaks and other trees, but even these are not seen in all their beauty, for more often than not they are almost lost in thickets of self-sown undergrowth.

There are, however, plans in course of preparation for extensive alterations to the pleasure grounds at Woburn, for, extensive as they are, they do lack the interest of the many trees and shrubs now available. Formerly, when there were not the many richly varied, ornamental flowering and foliage trees and shrubs which we now have, choice was limited. There were box, laurels and yews and a limited number of not particularly interesting flowering subjects. The ancient cedars, oaks and beeches are there, but two things are lacking. The greater number of the finer specimen trees do not stand, as they should, isolated in open spaces of lawn, so that their full beauty can be seen, and the grounds are without the more intimate loveliness of skilfully planned glades of ornamental flowering and foliage shrubs and trees.

The potential grandeur exists but the softer, more intimate loveliness has to be created. It should be interesting to the many visitors to Woburn Abbey to watch both the increasingly interesting collection of plants, and perhaps even more the development of the pleasure grounds into the lovely glades that are being planned for their enjoyment.

There are also in course of preparation plans for a Japanese garden. If carried out, this would be not only very interesting in itself but a complete change from the formal gardens and glades.

In their main idea the new designs for the gardens at Woburn, shown on page 24, show a formal garden, slightly sunken and in three divisions, the divisions turning sharply at right angles. The principal turning point is a square garden with a water basin and fountain marking the focal point. This garden by its formality and the richness of its planting will be a complete change from the informal but lovely lines of the glade. The formal garden, both in its design, its straight lines and the brilliance of its colouring, would be in strong contrast to the softly curving lines of the glade borders. And yet each from this contrast makes the other so much more interesting. The cedars and many very fine trees already existing will be as far as possible left standing in open stretches of lawn so that they will be seen in all their beauty.

Increasing the horticultural interest of the glade the designs show in the more open spaces flowering trees and shrubs, such as philadelphus, cytisus, prunus, weigela, deutzias,

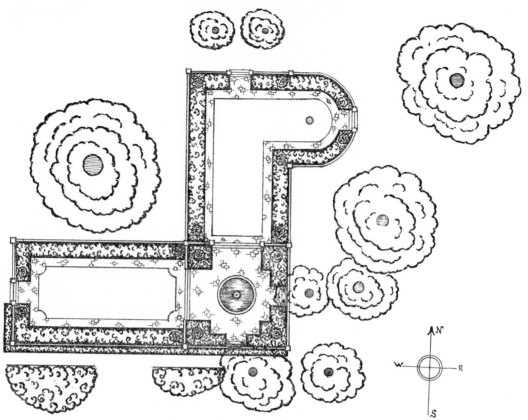

Design for new formal gardens at Woburn Abbey

berberis, buddleias, ribes and many others. These shrubs would be as far as possible planted in groups, each group consisting of the finer varieties of the particular genus. The different varieties of a genus often seem to have an underlying affinity so that they may be used together to make large and attractive groups.

Of trees there are *Sequoia sempervirens, Taxodium distichum* (the swamp cypress) near one of the lakes, groups of *Quercus ilex,* an exceptionally fine weeping copper beech, and *Carpinus betulus* (hornbeam).

With so much that is good of the original design, to which will be related the newer glade borders enriched with the more recent additions of flowering and evergreen trees and shrubs, the union of old and new in the pleasure grounds at Woburn Abbey should result in something exceptionally fine.

# Flowering Plants and Herbaceous Borders

WHEN SPRING and early summer trees and shrubs have finished flowering and the delicate fresh greens of spring foliage have turned to the more sombre tones of midsummer, gardens should not become masses of dark rhododendrons and dull-looking shrubs. They should continue lovely with colour into and through the long summer days and well into the autumn, and this is when roses and herbaceous plants come into their own.

Flowering plants can be used to give the final glory of colour to gardens in many ways. Herbaceous borders can be in various shades of one colour, say from cream to deepest yellow or orange; blue borders are refreshingly cool in appearance and clear blues in a green setting can be delightful; a border of grey-foliage plants with perhaps only pink and white flowers could be charming; blue, purple and grey, too, would be distinctive, and borders of strong colours—reds, purples and oranges—could be striking in their almost oriental brilliance. Plants and flowers can be used to give endless harmonies of colour.

## Special borders

When space allows some plants, paeonies for instance, could be given a border to themselves. Paeonies take two years to become established, but a paeony border in all shades of white, cream, from pale to deep pink, reds and crimsons, can be lovely. Even after they have finished flowering their bronze-green foliage is decorative and fairly wide borders could be planted with two or three rows of paeonies in front and two or more rows of some later flowering plants behind them. Asters (Michaelmas daisies) in all their shades of mauves, blues, pinks, crimsons and purples, will by themselves make lovely colour schemes, soft but rich, and they could, in a wide border, be planted behind the earlier flowering paeonies.

## Iris gardens

Irises, too, can be grown by themselves either in an iris border or in a separate garden. Their grey-green, swordlike leaves look particularly well against flagstones and a paved iris garden can be a joy when the irises are flowering, and even later their foliage is decorative. Like most plants with grey foliage they grow best in soil with a high lime content, but the basic nature of the soil is of no great importance as lime can always be added. Blues, as distinct from mauves and purples, are particularly useful and have a colour value entirely their own. Mulberry-coloured irises are distinctive and tone especially well with pale yellow and chrome varieties. Of yellow iris, Lady Mohr, Pinnacle, Rocket, St Crispin, Yellow Hercules and Xantha, this last with large flowers of rich deep yellow, are all good. But there are so many excellent varieties that it is invidious to name a few. Skilfully planted there are more than enough to make an iris border or garden a charming sight. Iris should be planted with the upper part of the rhizome exposed to sun and air.

## Blue borders

Delphiniums in all shades of blue and purple are the glory of midsummer flower gardens. Their stately spires, planted at regular intervals down the length of a herbaceous border, give an idea of order that can be very satisfying and blue in its many tones goes happily with most other colours. A border of delphiniums only can be charming and they can, too, be planted in groups amongst shrubs, but planted in this way there should be sufficient to make an impact, say a dozen or more to a group. As an example, their blue shades seem to take on an added loveliness against a background of *Cotoneaster franchetii*, the grey, not very exciting flowers and downy undersides of the cotoneaster leaves being a perfect foil for the blues of the delphiniums.

## Yellow and golden gardens

In yellow or golden gardens, yellow anthemis with the taller creamy-white *Artemisia lactiflora* behind it would be charming. *Thalictrum glaucum* with plumes of greenish-yellow flowers; *Helenium autumnale pumilum magnificum*, a deep butter yellow; and coreopsis, of which there are several good varieties, could be included. Such a garden should be in full sun as in sunlight yellows and golds gleam like silk. Yellow and white hollyhocks, too, if white may be admitted into a yellow garden, are lovely together. Their flowers are a kind of paper white rather like *Romneya coulteri*. Both the single and double forms can be included, although personally I like the single ones better. Hollyhocks look their best against a tall hedge or wall and they need lower plants in front of them to hide their bare stems. For this purpose, in a golden garden, floribunda roses, such as Allgold or Poulsen's Yellow, both of which tone beautifully with almost any other colour and flower continuously, would make charming colour harmonies. Sunflowers and solidago or Golden Rod—the strong growing variety Golden Wings and the newer shorter kinds Leraft and Lemore—prolong the flowering season of yellow or golden borders or gardens. Groups of *Lilium testaceum* or *L. tigrinum*, too, would heighten the colour values and there are the shrubby hypericums which produce their pleasing yellow flowers over a long period.

## White gardens

One scarcely realises how many shades of white there are until one comes to use them. Of lilies, *L. candidum* and *L. regale* are unrivalled for scent, as, too, for the delicate beauty of their flowers, and once established they are easy to grow. As backgrounds there could be philadelphus in its many varieties, most of them fragrant and lasting in flower well into the summer. The paper-white *Romneya coulteri* with the loveliest shade of soft yet deep gold centres; Shasta daisies, single and double; and hostas (funkias) could be included, both for their grey-green leaves, which go so beautifully with white flowers and for their silvery-lilac blooms. Hostas make an excellent foil for white lilies. Amongst shrubs with white flowers there are *Cytisus albus*, *Cistus cyprius* with a maroon blotch at the base of the petals, and *C. corbariensis* with a yellow flush. There are, too, *Escallonia iveyi*, evergreen with white flowers, and *Choisya ternata*, the glossy evergreen foliage of which is fragrant when crushed. And there are spiraeas and white roses for the back.

## Phlox borders

A border of phlox in their many shades from pale to deepest pink, orange, scarlet, deep purple, mauve and white give rich masses of colour and they are at their best during August and September when delphiniums and the earlier herbaceous plants have finished flowering. Phlox, which like a cool, moist soil but plenty of sun, planted in herbaceous borders, would lengthen the flowering season.

## Shrubs in herbaceous borders

To save work a number of shrubs could well be included in herbaceous borders (Plate 6). The shrubs should be if possible summer flowering and they must fit harmoniously into the colour scheme. For this purpose grey foliage is particularly useful. Because of its grey leaves *Senecio laxifolius* with yellow flowers tones happily with most colours, and it has a delightful habit of growing down over a wall face when planted in raised pockets or on the top of a retaining wall. *Phlomis fruticosa* is somewhat similar, only with flowers of a slightly orange shade. Floribunda roses, too, are useful and can be chosen to fit into any colour scheme. They continue to flower throughout the summer and being permanent, save a lot of work. Groups of Floribunda roses should be proportional to the size of the border, but it is essential to have enough plants in each group to seem an integral part of the planting. Yet another effective way of using these roses is to plant a part of a border with perennials using the roses and other shrubs towards one or both ends. In this case the change from herbaceous plants to more shrubs or roses should not be too abrupt.

Amongst summer-flowering shrubs suitable for inclusion in herbaceous borders is *Abelia chinensis* with clusters of white flowers flushed with pink and flowering from July onwards. Abelias should be given a reasonably sheltered place. The silvery-grey foliage of *Artemisia arborescens* would earn it a place in any border, particularly with a grey or blue colour scheme. *Buddleia alternifolia* with its long racemes of mauve flowers would be distinctive with purple delphiniums or I often plant it next to the pink flowered *Escallonia* Apple Blossom or the newer *E.* Peach Blossom. *Buddleia alternifolia* is free growing and should be at the back where its pendulous habit would show beautifully. Ceanothus, too, in their charming shades of powder and deeper blues are suitable and *Ceratostigma willmottianum* with bright blue flowers from July onwards is indispensable for the front. *Choisya ternata*, the Mexican orange blossom, would give a useful touch of evergreen and its white flowers would be right with any colours.

Cistus in their different varieties could almost furnish a border but they are at their best on a dry wall or bank in full sun. To name two or three only, *Cistus corbariensis*, white with a yellow flush, is one of the hardiest; *C. purpureus*, red with a deeper red blotch in the centre, has large flowers and is one of the finest; while *C.* Silver Pink, although not quite so hardy, is a gem that should be in any collection. *C. cyprius*, the finest of the tall hardy varieties, grows to a height of from 6 to 8 feet and flowers continuously. There are, too, *C. loretii*, white with a crimson blotch; and the cistus relative, *Halimium ocymoides*, which produces small bright yellow flowers with a chocolate ring at their base.

*Cytisus battandieri* with yellow flowers, unusual both in colour and shape, is tall and at its best against a sunny wall. *Spartium junceum*, the Spanish broom, produces clouds of flowers of a pleasing shade of yellow during summer. Hibiscus, in shades of blue, mauve and white are distinctive, and the newer variety Woodbridge, a large-flowered single red, is well worth a place. There are, too, hypericums, the choicer varieties of which are some of the best of summer-flowering shrubs. *H. patulum forrestii* has large golden yellow flowers and its autumn foliage, a rich deep shade, is very decorative. *H. moserianum* is dwarf and spreading, a useful plant for the front, while *H.* Rowallane, attaining a height of up to 4 feet, is one of the finest of the genus.

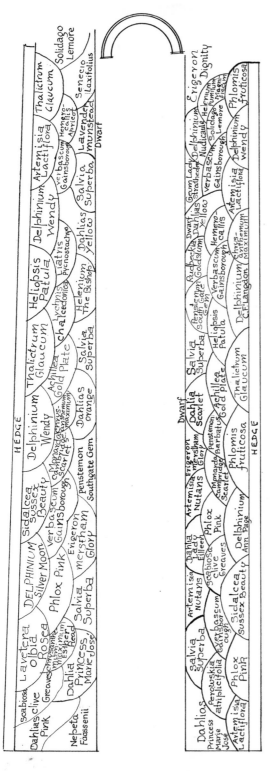

Plan for flower border giving a definite colour scheme

Planting plan for border containing chiefly shrubs to give the effect of an herbaceous border

Growing up to 5 feet in height, *Olearia haastii*, decorative itself, is useful because the grey-white flowers with which it is covered enhance the values of any flowers near it. *Olearia macrodonta* grows well near the sea and *O. scilloniensis* is another good variety. Perovskia, the Russian Sage, which should be planted in full sun, has blue flowers, very silvery deeply cut foliage and is invaluable. *Phlomis fruticosa* is another shrub with grey foliage that may be planted in such a border as I am describing. Like *Senecio laxifolius*, it has the useful habit of growing down over a wall face. Potentillas, too, of which there are several good varieties, produce their flowers in all shades of yellow and white over a long period. *Romneya coulteri*, the Californian Tree Poppy, can be included in any border, shrub or herbaceous; its paper-white flowers with yellow centres against very grey leaves are charming with the powder-blue *Ceanothus* Gloire de Versailles. *Romneya coulteri*, which is at its best against a south wall, also seems to enhance the value of any flowers near it.

The grey-green aromatic leaves of rosemary entitle it to a place both in herbaceous borders or with shrubs. *Santolina chamaecyparissus*, another dwarf shrub with very grey foliage, is useful for the front, rather more for its grey foliage than for its flowers, a not very pleasing shade of yellow. For the back of fairly wide borders *Holodiscus discolor ariaefolius*, attaining a height of 9 or 10 feet, produces drooping panicles of creamy-white flowers in midsummer. And there are several of the shrubby veronicas or hebes, amongst them *H.* Autumn Glory, low and with deep violet flowers; *H. traversii* producing a cloud of greyish-white flowers over its not particularly attractive foliage, is useful for the way in which it intensifies the value of adjacent colours. The plan on page 29 shows how a border may be planted chiefly with suitable shrubs and yet give very much the effect of a herbaceous border. The advantage of this predominant use of shrubs is that the planting is permanent and labour-saving as practically no staking would be necessary. To give rather more the effect of a herbaceous border a few groups of, say, delphiniums and phlox, both of which are, for their colour values, outstanding, might well be included.

*Colour arrangement*

The detailed planting plan for flower borders on page 29 is arranged to give a definite colour scheme. From nearest the house, as we may take it that it will generally be approached from that end, the border starts with pink, white, mauve, blue and grey. Gradually, imperceptibly, it changes to stronger colours—orange, purple, blue, yellow, crimson and scarlet—with again the relief of a few groups of plants with grey foliage. Towards the farther end, and again imperceptibly, the border changes to yellow, blue, grey and a little white. White flowers other than in a white garden, should be in very small groups or they may lessen the colour values too much.

The repetition of noticeably outstanding plants down the length of a herbaceous border gives a feeling of order and continuity. Blue is a colour that goes with nearly everything and in the plan on page 29 delphiniums are shown used in this way. Pink phlox and the grey foliage of perovskia with its clear blue flowers, and scabiosa against the pink dahlias Lady Aileen or Princess Marie Jose, all fit happily into the colour scheme. Farther down the border the colours become stronger. Deep yellows and blues, orange, scarlet and crimson together make a riot of colour almost oriental in its richness. *Phlomis fruiticosa*, with yellow flowers, is good alike with the paler shades of pink or with stronger reds and orange. It is lovely, too, with *Penstemon barbatus* (*Chelone barbata*) which in the plan is shown in front of it. *Verbascum* Gainsborough, which produces the softest and most pleasing yellow flowers, is introduced into the length of the border that is more particularly pink as it helps to unite the two ranges of colour.

Now we come to the strong central length of the border. Here is *Thalictrum glaucum*, a yellow that can be used effectively with almost any colour. There is *Heliopsis patula*, a strong and perhaps rather harsh yellow, but now we are definitely working up to strong colours. There is *Lychnis chalcedonica* with pillar-box red flowers against *Achillea* Gold Plate, with *Salvia superba* growing lower in front, a brilliant galaxy. Next to the salvias a group of orange dahlias against the blue *Delphinium* Wendy and the deep yellow *Achillea* Gold Plate would be striking. *Salvia superba*, the repetition of which adds richness to any colour scheme, appears again. Going on from here there is *Verbascum* Gainsborough and *Hemerocallis* Apricot with next to it the soft yet deep yellow of *Solidago* Lemore.

In the opposite border delphiniums, tall and stately, makes a pleasing balance between the two borders. Returning towards the house dwarf yellow dahlias extend almost into the middle of the border with *Verbascum* Gainsborough near them. Now we come to very much the same strength of colour as on the opposite side but continuing for a slightly longer distance. This strong grouping of colour is given by dwarf scarlet dahlias, *Penstemon* Southgate Gem, a ruby red which has the amiable quality of harmonising with any colours, *Achillea* Gold Plate, with *Penstemon barbatus* and *Monarda didyma* Cambridge Scarlet, together a grouping of the richest colour. From here the colours gradually soften to the blue-mauve *Scabiosa* Clive Greaves, the noticeably grey *Artemisia nutans*, satin-pink sidalceas, pink phlox—the phlox should not be too strong in colour—the lovely blue perovskia with very grey finely cut leaves, to end with a group of dwarf dahlias. Princess Marie José would be a suitable variety next to some *Salvia superba* and with the cream plumes of *Artemisia lactiflora* growing taller behind it.

$$\left\{\begin{array}{c} 2 \end{array}\right\}$$

# *Rose Gardens*

THE INTIMACY and privacy of an enclosed space—the restful symmetry of ordered beds, enriched by the many colours to be found in the roses of today—is as much a necessity in a garden scheme as is the study or library in a house. Gardens devoted to a particular flower have long been popular, and of them all the rose garden is the most in favour.

The spirit of peace and harmony which should pervade the formal rose garden comes of good design and conscious planning, and not of a haphazard collection of beds planted indiscriminately, or of commonplace ornament. The flowering periods of each variety, arrangement of colour and habit of growth, are some of the more important considerations. The design of the enclosure should be determined by the character of the site and by the general layout of the whole garden scheme. Every site contains in itself the elements of the design most suited to it, and these should be developed in the most effective way. Rose gardens on irregular sites may often be made more interesting than the familiar types by reason of their unusual planning.

*Formal design*

Rose gardens should, in general, be designed on some geometrical or formal plan, such as a circle, an octagon, a rectangle or a square (Plates 7 and 9). Since it may be desirable to grow as many of the good varieties as space will allow, the beds should not be too large in proportion, and yet each should give an effective mass of colour. In few cases should the beds be less than 6 to 8 feet in width. The paths, if turfed, should be sufficiently wide for the passage of a mowing machine and preferably not less than 4 feet (Plate 10). The centre of the garden may be emphasised by a figure in lead or stone, an old well-head or sundial (Plate 11) and, since the garden is filled with colour and scent and the charm which comes from the blending of these two, one or more seats, possibly on the centre lines of main paths, are essential.

Owing to their long flowering period and their many beautiful shades, hybrid tea roses,

5. The upper and middle terraces at Hascombe Court, Surrey

6. Herbaceous borders at Bowhill, Chichester, in which shrubs have been included

7. Rose garden at Busbridge Wood, Godalming, Surrey

which are seen at their best in an enclosed setting, are the most suitable for bedding purposes. It was a stroke of genius on the part of the hybridisers to cross the China tea with the hybrid perpetual, and so bring into being the many fine varieties of hybrid tea rose now available. Every year new varieties are introduced, and though some pass quickly out of favour, an embarrassingly large choice remains. The final selection of a good rose rests to a considerable extent with the buyer, and as fashions for colour change, so do roses and those varieties which fail to attract are gradually eliminated from nurserymen's stocks.

*ROSE GARDEN.*

Sketch to show formal rose garden with centre pool

Choice in the selection of suitable varieties is largely governed by personal taste, but certain qualifications should not be overlooked. The roses should possess good colour and shape, and some varieties should be included for their fragrance, but even more important than these attributes is habit of growth, foliage and continuity of flowering. The soil and the position in which roses are planted may affect length of blooming, but the perfect bedding rose is one that possesses fragrance, shapeliness, vigorous growth, a long flowering period, and, as far as possible, freedom from disease.

In planting, each bed should be filled with one variety only, and the rose garden should be planted to some definite and considered colour scheme. The resultant formality, if this is done, will more than compensate for any lack in number of varieties. Beds or borders of mixed roses have the quality of diversity, but they have little else to recommend them. In order, however, to include a greater number of varieties, a continuous rose border or

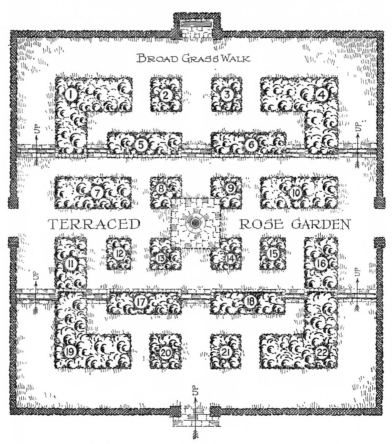

Plan for rose garden with grass walks. Suggested varieties, numbered on the plan, are as follows: (1) Josephine Bruce; (2, 3) Mischief; (4) Champs Elysées; (5) Dame Edith Helen; (6) Pink Perfume; (7) Belle Blonde; (8, 9) Baccara; (10) Sutter's Gold; (11) Golden Masterpiece; (12) McGredy's Ivory; (13, 14) Baccara; (15) Message; (16) Spek's Yellow; (17) Bettina; (18) Helen Traubel; (19) Christian Dior; (20, 21) Super Star; (22) Mardi Gras

borders might well be planted in different blocks of colour to some definite scheme. Many varieties introduced during the past few years have strong colours and it is advisable to separate such shades as orange and flame and bright pink, although with roses this separation is not quite so important as it would be, say, in a herbaceous border.

## Use of edging plants

In a paved rose garden, if violas and other suitable plants, grown as an edging to the beds, are encouraged to spread on to the paving and into its crevices, they will soften and give a charmingly furnished appearance (Plate 8). Blues, mauves, and soft pinks will tone with most rose colours. Suitable violas for this purpose are *V. cornuta purpurea*, Maggie Mott and

Plan for formal rose garden, paved, and with a central pool. Suitable varieties, numbered on the plan, are as follows: (1) Crimson Glory; (2) Picture; (3) Percy Thrower; (4) McGredy's Ivory; (5) Uncle Walter; (6) Madame Abel Chatenay; (7) Anne Watkins; (8) King's Ransom; (9) Belle Blonde; (10) Fragrant Cloud; (11) McGredy's Yellow; (12) Chrysler Imperial

Pickering Blue. The purple *V. c. purpurea* also blends beautifully with all the rose shades, as do several of the heucheras, their pink and rose shades toning so well with the rose growths and young red foliage. Clumps of pink, blue and purple, and silver-leaved paving plants such as acaena, *Achillea argentea*, and *Raoulia australis* can all be recommended, and the scent of roses will subtly blend with *Mentha requienii* and thyme. Should the garden be terraced out of a sloping lawn, any dry retaining walls can be covered with clinging wall plants. The dwarf *Phlox subulata*, whose mauves and pinks blend with any rose shades, *Dianthus gratianopolitanus* (*D. caesius*), the lovely blue *Campanula cochlearifolia* (*C. pusilla*), aubrietias for spring colour, helianthemums, and similar plants will inlay and mottle the weathering stone with delightful colour.

Other classes of bush roses that deserve mention, though not as popular as hybrid teas and perpetuals, are the single Irish varieties. These are a development of the hybrid teas which, since their appearance at the beginning of the century, have been developed into beautiful varieties. They have glossy foliage, a vigorous and hardy constitution, and they flower in their various colours of crimson, bronze, gold and shades of rose, continuously throughout the season. Messrs Alex Dickson and Son have produced such charming varieties as Irish Elegance, in shades of apricot, with buds of orange-scarlet, and Irish Fire-flame, an orange-copper rose, a more vivid variety of Irish Elegance.

Among the more suitable varieties for covering walls and fences are Allen Chandler, a vivid scarlet; Albertine, bright salmon; Dr W. Van Fleet, flesh pink; and The New Dawn, deep pink; these will clothe walls with curtains of the loveliest hues. The wich-uraiana roses and hybrids are excellent for pergolas and fences; two good varieties are Paul's Scarlet, a climber and Emily Gray, an excellent yellow rambler.

*Pergolas*

Nowhere do climbing and rambler roses look better than clothing the piers and cross timbers of a pergola, and a pergola can be a very attractive part of a rose garden (Plate 12). The piers should bear some resemblance to the house—piers of red brick would be right with a red brick house; stone piers with a stone house. Real York stone is expensive, but it is possible to obtain synthetic stones which, after they have weathered for a comparatively short time, are almost indistinguishable from real York. Marshalite, a synthetic stone made of York stone dust and cement, is very durable and is about half the cost of real York, an unusual combination of good qualities. It is obtainable in various sizes and it weathers to very much the appearance of York stone.

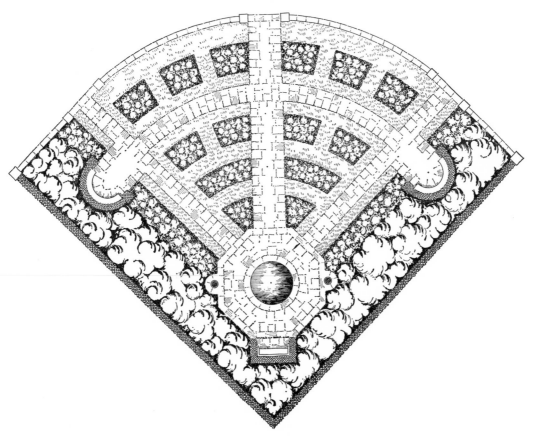

A pool is the focal point of this plan for a rose garden

## Floribunda roses

Although perhaps not quite right in formal rose gardens, floribunda roses may be relied on to give wonderful displays of colour through summer and autumn and, chosen with care, they can be almost as effective as bedding roses. Floribunda roses can be used in groups in herbaceous borders, where, as they need no staking, they are labour-saving and, suitably placed, they can be used to give effective groups of colour in glades during summer and autumn after the greater number of shrubs have finished flowering.

There are so many excellent varieties of roses from which to choose that to give names would serve little purpose, and there are new introductions every year. The following is, however, a short list of a few reliable kinds.

37

## Hybrid Tea Roses

### PINK

| | |
|---|---|
| Dame Edith Helen | Rich pink with large blooms, true old rose scent. |
| Grace De Monaco | Free-flowering, richly scented and of good branching habit. |
| Picture | Flowering over a long period, its glowing pink contrasts well with its bluish-green foliage. |
| Pink Favorite and Royalist | Rose-pink, particularly free-flowering and strongly disease resistant. |
| Prima Ballerina | Very fragrant deep pink with dark foliage. |

### RED AND CRIMSON

| | |
|---|---|
| Baccara | Full orange-red blooms on long stiff stems. |
| Champs Elysées | Rich red with good foliage, even habit of growth and flowering almost continuously. |
| Christian Dior | Strong-growing, of particularly fine form, free-flowering. |
| Ena Harkness | Free-flowering, crimson-scarlet, fine foliage and retains its colour. |
| Madame Louise Laperrière | Deep crimson with very rich scent. |
| Papa Meilland | Rich velvety crimson, outstandingly fragrant, large blooms. |

### YELLOW

| | |
|---|---|
| Belle Blonde | Richly scented, golden-yellow, shapely blooms well set off by glossy foliage. |
| McGredy's Yellow | Richly scented, buttercup-yellow, unfailingly strong-growing. |
| Peace | Long-flowering delicate yellow, edged with palest pink, very hardy, particularly fine foliage and growth habit. |
| Sun Valley | Very fragrant, its purity of colour contrasting well with its rich dark foliage. |
| Sutter's Gold | Unusually strongly perfumed for a yellow rose, very vigorous in habit. |

### WHITE AND CREAM

| | |
|---|---|
| Innocence | Sweetly scented single rose. |
| Marcia Stanhope | Of vigorous growth and sweetly scented. |
| McGredy's Ivory | Large creamy-white blooms, freely produced, excellent bedder. |
| Virgo | Well shaped blooms of pure white. |

**VERMILION**
Super Star — Unfading self-colour, of perfect form and sweetly scented. Free-flowering, hardy and disease resistant.

**ORANGE**
Mojave — Deep orange blooms freely produced, bright green foliage.
Soraya — Orange-red, strong-growing and free-flowering, large-flowered variety.

**BICOLOURS**
Silver Lining — Silvery-rose, free-flowering and richly scented.
Talisman and Tzigane — Two of the best red and yellow combinations, vigorous growth, Talisman having the advantage of strong scent.

## Floribunda Roses

**YELLOW**
Allgold — Perhaps the best deep yellow, free-flowering even in the driest weather.

Golden Fleece — Richly scented, retaining its colour into maturity.

**PINK**
Else's Rival — Carmine-pink, making a solid mass of bloom, very compact growth.

Fashion — Salmon-pink with faintly scented double flowers.

**RED**
Donald Prior — Semi-double rich blood-red, retains its colour.
Lilli Marlene — Free-flowering and long-lasting, fully double with very fine foliage.

Moulin Rouge — Of vigorous growth, semi-double and unfading, very attractive in bud stage.

**ORANGE**
Orangeade and Orange Sensation — Both semi-doubles of vigorous growth and vivid colouring.

**WHITE**
Irene of Denmark, Iceberg and Ivory Fashion — All vigorous growers, Irene of Denmark and Ivory Fashion being scented.

## Climbing and Rambling Roses

| | |
|---|---|
| Albertine | Salmon-pink, fading at the edge, very early flowering. |
| Dr Van Fleet | Flesh pink, very glossy foliage with larger flowers than ordinary ramblers. |
| Gloire de Dijon | Often in flower in May and continuing until late in the year. One of the best of the old climbers, soft yellow flowers with good scent. |
| Lemon Pillar | Creamy-yellow, single, from June to October. |
| Paul's Scarlet | Rich scarlet, continuous flowering period. |

## Climbing Sports

| | |
|---|---|
| Climbing Ena Harkness | Red, well shaped flowers of vigorous growth. |
| Lady Hillingdon | Apricot-yellow, attaining a greater height than most. |
| Mme Abel Chatenay | Pink, one of the oldest and best of its colour. |
| Mme Alfred Carrière | White, reliable for a north aspect, very fragrant, flowers both in summer and autumn. |
| Shot Silk | Deep rosy-gold, flowering again in the autumn. |
| Spek's Yellow | Deep yellow, particularly good in bud. |

All the climbing sports of the hybrid teas have an advantage over other climbers and ramblers in that they need only very light pruning.

8. The rose garden and lily pool at Westfields, Bedfordshire

9. Monteviot, near Jedburgh; the rose garden in the foreground

10. Rose garden at Ridge End, Worcestershire

11. Rose beds in a formal paved garden at Hillside, Four Oaks, Warwickshire

12. Pergola flanking tennis court at Boden's Ride, Ascot, Berkshire

# 3

# Water Gardens

WINDING THROUGH trees, tumbling over grey rocks, and widening into sunlit or dark still pools, running water will, by its freshness, its shadowy depths and its reflections, add more to the enchantment of a garden than many more pretentious features.

The presence of water also means that the many moisture-loving plants can be grown under conditions most suited to their needs, and that consequently they will attain their full beauty. There is all the difference between such plants grown in the damp soil bordering some natural stream or pool, and the same plants grown in an ordinary border, no matter how carefully they may be watered and tended.

But the greatest value of water lies in its light, its reflections, the feeling of space that it gives, and the contrast of its level surface with the varying outlines of its banks and the heights and reflections of the surrounding trees and planting.

Naturally making its way through the lowest levels, an existing stream could be widened here and there into pools. Boulders of stone could be used to retain its banks, not too obviously or too generously, for they should seem to be natural to, and not to have been built into, their places. Should there be a supply of water near enough to allow a hydraulic ram to be used, a ram which will pump up a reasonable stream of water, enough to make the ground wet round the pool, one could, with dams and sluices, widen a stream into the semblance of a lake, smaller or larger as the contours of the ground and the supply of water make possible, and in this connection it will be recognised that a bulldozer or grab, hired for the job, can cost far less in proportion to rising costs than the army of navvies Capability Brown could lay on.

Small ponds mean mosquitoes, real lakes good fishing and skating, and where the ground has the right contours, a lake is cheaper than a rock garden. I am thinking of large gardens, but remember that you do not have to weed water, only occasionally clean it out and this can be done during a spell of dry weather.

## Construction of streams and pools

When making an artificial watercourse the channel should first be dug and roughly shaped. It should be given a pleasingly irregular outline, but this will probably be determined to some degree by the contours of the ground. It may be necessary to concrete small pools, in which case it must be remembered that the soil at the edges of the pool or stream will be as dry as other parts of the garden. In any case the concrete sides should be hidden as far as possible with stones, turf or overgrowing planting.

After the channel and pools are excavated, their beds and sides should be covered with about 6 inches of concrete, which should be scratched before it sets, to take a final rendering, half an inch in thickness, of a strong mixture of sand and cement. For large pools the concrete should be proportionately thicker—up to 8 or 9 inches, and its beds should be reinforced with steel rods or expanded metal. The thickness of the rods, which should be laid crossing each other so that they form a pattern of squares, will vary according to the bearing quality of the soil and the size of the pools; $\frac{3}{8}$ inch would be an average thickness, but on light or moving soils, as also in larger pools, they could be $\frac{1}{2}$ or even $\frac{5}{8}$ of an inch in diameter.

## Choice and use of rock

The artistry which results in the making of a beautiful informal water garden consists chiefly in outlining its banks, in placing any stones where they tell to the best advantage, and in its planting. Proportionally large stones must be used. They should be firmly fixed in concrete where this is necessary for security and, in places, flat ones should be laid to project over the water, giving mysterious shadows and shelter for any fish that may be introduced into the pools.

A stream or pool, or any comparatively small sheet of water, can easily be brought into the general scheme and can be given the decorative planting of the garden proper. If the outlines of the banks are not good these should be altered by forming here and there an inlet or bay and by extending any slight projection farther into the water. To do this, stout stakes should be driven in to retain the soil of the extended parts, the spaces between the stakes and the land being filled with the soil from the bays as they are dug.

## Planting banks

In some cases there should be borders or planting on both sides of the mown grass near the water, and, amongst the shrubs which are planted to furnish and define it, bold masses of suitable moisture-loving perennials would give colour and interest during summer and autumn. *Lobelia cardinalis* Queen Victoria, with flowers of glowing crimson crowning its wine-red stems and leaves, will give the richest colour, but it is not perfectly hardy and must be lifted each autumn to be replanted the following spring. The crimson flowered *Monarda didyma* Cambridge Scarlet, also moisture-loving and hardy, would grow well in moist soil. Astilbes and herbaceous spiraeas should be in damp ground close to the water. The deep rose and red shades of the astilbes Granat and *gloria purpurea* are particularly good. The tall, white plumes of *Aruncus sylvester*, which also should be near the water, have the luxuriant appearance belonging to so many moisture-loving plants. Herbaceous phlox like moist places, and in their range of colours from rich salmons to soft pinks, mauves and purples, are very suitable for rather damp, but not wet, borders. Although they do better not exposed to full sunshine, and like copious supplies of water, phlox are not for boggy places. Sidalceas and the purple heads of eupatoriums, too, look well with *Macleaya cordata*, a stately perennial with attractive glaucous foliage.

Planting by streamlets or by smaller pools again depends on the character of their surroundings. *Primula japonica* and its hybrids in shades of pink and red, together with *Iris sibirica* and *I. kaempferi* are some of the most suitable of moisture-loving plants for such places. *Primula pulverulenta* with whorl upon whorl of deep claret coloured flowers; *P. bulleyana*, with terracotta, apricot and orange-yellow flowers; *P. sikkimensis*, a Himalayan introduction, with soft yellow delightfully scented flowers; and another yellow variety *P. helodoxa* are, when planted in groups, some of the most effective of the family.

The beautiful Japanese *Iris kaempferi* will grow to perfection by the stream side; the Siberian flag, *I. sibirica*, its variety *orientalis*, and the rosy-lilac flowered *I. laevigata*, are invaluable for the delicacy of their colouring, and their formal grace. Other interesting subjects for smaller planting are the golden marsh marigold, *Caltha palustris*, and the tall yellow loosestrife, *Lysimachia punctata*, both of which delight in wet places, but which must be separated from plants with deep pink flowers. The rose-coloured astilbes, orange and yellow trollius, mimulus, and hostas, will grow vigorously in full sun, while for partial shade trilliums, and the intense blue *Omphalodes cappadocica*, gleam as starlight in a dark sky.

When the stream is fed by surface springs and the surrounding ground is consequently marshy there is a wide choice of plants. The sapphire blue *Aquilegia glandulosa*; the willow gentian, *Gentiana asclepiadea*, with its large blue trumpets on arching stems; *Cypripedium reginae*, Lady's Slipper, one of the best of our native orchids; and *Mertensia virginica*, are all invaluable for this type of garden. These should all be planted to look as if growing naturally.

Some plants—the diminutive reed, *Acorus gramineus pusillus*, and the flowering rush, *Butomus umbellatus*—should have their rootstocks submerged in shallow water. In the same category can be classed the familiar water forget-me-nots and kingcups, those common but none the less beautiful wild flowers. *Sagittaria latifolia*, a handsome variety of the water plantain family; *Typha angustifolia*, or Reed Mace; and the pink-flowered *Alisma plantago-aquatica* should all be planted in 1 foot of water, and are useful for beautifying the banks of streams or of small pools in the bog garden.

A stream flows through the centre of the rock garden at Hascombe Court. It is made on steeply sloping ground, the water falling from the highest level through a succession of pools into a larger pool at the lowest level. As the soil is very light and sandy and has no retentive properties, the pools, constructed of Westmorland water-worn stone, are set in concrete. If a rock or water garden is to look natural the stones should be proportionately large and in their placing they should conform to their natural stratification, that is, each stone should be laid on its natural bed. At Hascombe Court the general curvature of the rock-bound water channel creates to some extent the illusion that it is part of a mountain stream.

## Alterations

To consider larger sheets of water, sometimes an existing pool, when it is fed by springs or running water, can be enlarged, possibly into the semblance of a lake. It could be deepened, but except in the case of a bathing-pool, from 2 to 3 feet would be a sufficient depth, and on a retentive soil, puddling, or hard ramming of the bottom for consolidation, might be the only treatment necessary.

Because of the gently sloping ground comparatively little stone was used in the water gardens at Westwoods, Plate 14, and at Westfields, Plate 15, but every care was taken to obtain rhythm of line and balance in its arrangement. The overflow from an upper pool falls over blocks of water-worn Westmorland stone into the lower larger pool. The stones, so lovely in themselves, seem to belong naturally to the gardens.

Any planting of trees and shrubs must be proportional to the extent of the water and its setting, and the character of such planting will, to some extent, be governed by the situation of the water and the outline of its banks. A lake, or fairly large sheet, will require large trees grouped boldly in suitable places on or near its banks, and even the smaller and more decorative planting should be in proportionally large groups, or it will not tell from a distance. It should be remembered, too, that in most cases it is the planting on the opposite bank that is seen and appreciated most.

## Developing vistas

To extend, where possible, existing vistas across a lake, and into or through the planting on the farther side, would increase their effect immensely. The choice of trees will be governed very largely by the nature of the soil, but they should be grouped to frame, and not to obstruct, the vistas. A comfortably wide stretch of turf could be left surrounding, and in places coming down to the water's edge. In others there can be groups of moisture-loving plants between the turf and water. Softer colours do not tell so well from a distance whereas good masses of red or of reds and purples growing on the opposite banks and reflected in the water would be most effective. Rhododendrons used to this end would give banks and pools of richest colour.

Dignity and grandeur of scenery should go with extensive water, and these qualities come from forest trees growing high and prominent in the landscape, from masses of rhododendrons or other suitable plants growing down to the water's surface, so that flowers and reflections meet. Where space allows, conifers or deciduous trees could be planted, or both. Seen in perspective, as they would be when looking down the length of a vista, specimen trees standing singly or in groups could frame broad ways into the distance. Any decorative planting of garden shrubs or flowers would be out of place near large sheets of water in parkland, or in natural scenery, but there could well be drifts of purple loosestrife or other moisture-loving wild flowers. Forest trees and wild flowers can be surprisingly beautiful when the wild flowers are in sufficient numbers.

There is a distinct difference between grandeur and beauty, and just as grandeur comes of wide spaces and long distance, and height in proportion, beauty belongs to more sophisticated scenes, and can be created in smaller spaces. Its component parts can be more varied and ornamental, and garden shrubs and flowers with which to make it can be used.

As with gardens, so will straight lines and obvious boundaries have the effect of apparently restricting the extent of water, just as, on the other hand, skilfully planned curving lines of banks and skilful planting can be made apparently to increase it. One or more weeping willows on an island, or on the mainland, can be arranged to give shadow and distance to water beyond, so that it appears to extend almost indefinitely.

## Trees for the waterside

Amongst Scots pines and silver birches the banks, on suitable soil, may be planted with irregularly placed clumps of rhododendrons or pontica azaleas, which, in common with many other plants, like and do well in moist ground. Weeping willows, although they will, as a matter of fact, grow very well elsewhere, really belong to the waterside, and *Salix alba tristis*, the golden weeping willow, a beautiful tree, could be planted where its pendulous branches will break any unnatural lines of an artificially formed pool. *S. babylonica*—there are few trees more effective in winter—should be planted to give bold effects near larger sheets of water. Such types as *S. vitellina*, with golden branches, and *S. v. britzensis*, with stems of orange-red, are even more vivid if cut back each year in late winter. Other varieties with, in early spring, silvery catkins which later turn golden, are the native *Salix caprea*, or palm willow, so useful for indoor decoration, and *S. daphnoides*, a handsome species with larger catkins on red stems overlaid with a bluish bloom.

Familiarity sometimes dulls our perceptions, and the beauty of some of the common wild trees and plants is not always recognised. Because of their graceful and rapid growth the varieties of the common alder are valuable for furnishing banks quickly. If the surroundings are extensive, or lawns sweep down to the waterside, poplars, *Populus nigra* and *P. alba*, and the aspen may not be out of scale, but these ultimately become too large for smaller gardens. Again, if space permits, *Taxodium distichum*, the swamp cypress, will grow well either with its roots submerged or on the surrounding banks. Its rich brown trunk and soft green foliage, changing later to red-brown, with its pyramidal form, make this a tree of marked distinction.

There are many trees and shrubs suitable for planting in less swampy conditions. Rowans grow wild by mountain streams in the Lake District, their orange and scarlet berries telling clearly against the lichen-covered boulders. The beautiful North American snowdrop tree, *Halesia carolina*, the branchlets of which are hung in May with pendant white bell-like flowers, should be more extensively planted near water as it enjoys a moist loam but it does dislike lime. Few shrubs also are more suitable for waterside planting than our native guelder rose, *Viburnum opulus*, and, remarkable for their vivid leaf tints, *V. tomentosum plicatum* and *V. opulus sterile* are at their best with their branches, pendulous with the weight of white ball-like flowers, hanging over water. In a mass, the stems of *Cornus alba* Westonbirt, decorative even in summer, will glow red in winter sunshine, provided they are cut hard back just before growth commences in the spring. Some wax-white-stemmed brambles, such as *Rubus cockburnianus*, would be very beautiful near them.

Although not actually water-loving plants, many of the stronger-growing species of roses would do well in the surrounding planting or overhanging the stream. The crimson foliage and stems of *Rosa rubrifolia* tone beautifully with the pink inflorescence of *Spiraea douglasii*, which makes a striking patch of purplish-rose, that is if enough are planted in the one group. Scarcely can there be too many spiraeas, so suitable are their feathery plumes and handsome foliage for waterside planting. One of the finest, now known as *Sorbaria aitchisonii*, produces large panicles of white flowers and attains a height of up to 10 feet in favourable positions.

## Perennials for moist soils

The yellow and apricot shades of hemerocallis; the late-flowering *Primula florindae*, and the blue and violet *Aconitum wilsonii*, or *A. fischeri*, can be grouped with the soft pinks of sidalceas with delightful results. Stronger yellows and oranges, such as are to be found in the flowers of *Ligularia clivorum*, are effective for massed planting and tell well from a distance. But oranges and the deeper yellows must be kept well away from any shade of rose-pink. Rodgersias with their bronze-green, cut leaves are strikingly handsome growing close to or spreading over water. *R. pinnata* changes to rich red in the autumn, and, with its deep pink flowers, will always add distinction to waterside planting. The luxuriant leaves and flowers of *Rheum palmatum* make its inclusion imperative where space allows. Rheums, and gunneras, too, with their enormous leaves, will give something of a tropical quality to any planting of which they form a part.

*Formal water gardens*

I have been writing of informal or natural water gardens, but a formal water garden can be one of the most beautiful adjuncts to any garden scheme. Its charm would depend almost entirely on good proportions, balanced stretches of green lawn, possibly walks of paving, and the right choice of ornament (Plates 13 and 16). Often flower borders can be dispensed with altogether and colour provided by shrubs such as *Ceanothus veitchianus, C.* Gloire de Versailles and climbing roses, by standard flowering crabs and cherries, scattering their pink and white petals on green turf and grey stone, and by water-lilies opening their waxen cups on the still water.

# 4

# *Glades*

No PART of the garden is easier to make and to maintain, nor can be lovelier, than a well-designed and carefully planted glade of trees and shrubs.

Glades may be made on level or on sloping ground; they may be small or they may be extensive. Usually a garden glade consists of a lawn bordered with shrubs and trees, so arranged that each shrub or tree, or group of shrubs or trees, can attain its own characteristic beauty of form and foliage, in addition to helping in the most effective way towards the ultimate beauty of the glade as a whole.

## *Different types*

There are garden glades and there are woodland glades. A woodland glade is, as its name implies, a clearing in or through a wood probably beyond the boundaries of the garden proper (Plate 20). A garden glade is a lawn, probably varying in width and with its curving borders planted chiefly with flowering trees and shrubs (Plate 17). There is all the difference between the two.

One way in which the modern garden—I am writing of comparatively small gardens—differs from the gardens of earlier times is that both formality and informality are woven into the same design; each by its contrast enhancing the value of the other. A small but beautiful glade can easily be made in a garden of, say, three-quarters of an acre in extent, it is a question of keeping everything in it to scale. One tree or shrub that is too large can dwarf the whole garden.

In many gardens there is ground, it may be small, it may be more extensive, which can, by the skilful use of curving borders, be made into a glade. And if such ground twists and turns so that one does not know what to expect round the next corner the element of surprise will add to its charm. Indeed in any garden, if the terrace, rose garden or whatever formal parts may go to make the whole, are proportional in themselves, in their relation

48

to the garden as a whole and are set in an informal glade, also proportionally right, then an interesting and beautiful garden will result.

## Backgrounds for planting

Like pictures hanging on a wall rather than, if one can imagine it, hanging in space, the shrubs in glade borders will look finer and grow better if they are seen against the density and protection of a hedge (Plate 19). For boundary hedges *Chamaecyparis lawsoniana* would be suitable or instead there are *C. l. allumii* and *C.* Triomphe de Boskoop. For heavier soils *Thuja lobii* would be suitable and *Cuppressocyparis leylandii* can be recommended for its toughness and quick rate of growth. *C. lawsoniana allumii*, with pleasing grey-green foliage, would be right with any colours; *C.* Triomphe de Boskoop is wider and darker than *C. l. allumii* and makes an excellent background.

Beech, thorn, holly or myrobalan plum are suitable hedging plants. Holly is excellent, but it is rather expensive and grows very slowly. Beech and myrobalan, on the other hand, both grow fairly quickly and are comparatively inexpensive. Quickthorn alone, or thorn and common privet together, always seem right with rural surroundings, and *Chamaecyparis lawsoniana* soon makes a good dense evergreen hedge. Alternatively, boundary hedges could be dispensed with and more conifers and evergreens planted at the back of the borders.

## Continuity of interest

More than any other part of the garden, because the foundation of their beauty is form, glades of trees and shrubs can be beautiful throughout the year. In early spring the young buds break on deciduous branches, lace-like against the dark greens of firs, spruce, holly or other trees with evergreen foliage. Towards the end of January its closely set flowers star the branches of *Hamamelis mollis*, and later forsythias turn golden with blooms on all the length of their stems. Then quickly lilacs and laburnums, cherries, azaleas, rhododendrons, spiraeas, and other spring-flowering trees and shrubs turn into banks and cascades of blossom.

Afterwards follow the summer and autumn-flowering subjects. There are not so many of these, but their flowers tell to the greater advantage amidst the surrounding green, red and purple foliage. During summer, too, flower borders and rose gardens are filled with colour, and the change from these to the cool verdure of a glade of trees and shrubs is welcome, each heightening, by its contrast, the beauty of the others.

In autumn and winter, glades remain the most interesting parts of the garden. Many of the deciduous berberis take on wonderful colours; colours which last well into winter.

Japanese maples change to a greater brilliance of reds and flames. Azaleas shed their leaves in dying splendour. *Cercidiphyllum japonicum* becomes a rich claret. On crabs and thorns, fruit and berries hang thickly, and the whole garden is resplendent. Scarcely have the last colours faded, before the earliest leaves and flowers of another year are opening.

## Preparations for planting

Borders in which trees and shrubs are to be planted should be dug deeply with the same thoroughness that should be given to other parts of the garden. Any rough grass or turf that is not required for the making of new lawns should be chopped with the spade into small pieces and dug into the lower spit. In addition, most of the deciduous shrubs and trees—lilacs, weigelas, cherries, crabs—should have a moderate dressing of well-decayed manure dug into the borders before they are planted. If this is done, and the soil is in a suitable condition, trees and shrubs should grow vigorously from the start, and make shapely bushes and trees within a comparatively short space of time.

## Shrubs for poorer soil

There are, however, a number of shrubs, which colour and berry much more effectively in poor and light, rather than in heavier and richer soils. Most of the berberis family should be grown in conditions exposed to full sun and in poor ground. They will, in fact, do well on dry banks, as long as the ground is properly dug. *Berberis thunbergii*, to take an example, seen in full sunlight, will wake up the garden with its autumn splendour of fiery crimson, while in shade or in a north border it may possibly fail to colour altogether.

The number of shrubs available is legion, and, a convenient fact, glades can be small or extensive and they can be planned to suit any site. Indeed, if any glade can curve in its length it will be so much finer than if it were straight. To consider planting, the more outstanding trees and taller shrubs should be placed first with due regard to balance of form and colour and, to consider evergreens, chamaecyparis whether singly or in groups should not be opposite each other. That is symmetry. They should be placed so that although not opposite, group or tree answers group or tree in such a way as to create a pleasing feeling of balance, and this balance should be continued for the length of the glade with all the taller and more noticeable trees and shrubs.

## Colour arrangement

Season of flowering, too, must be considered. To come to a group of forsythia, one of the finest of early flowering shrubs, opening, softly yellow, in a setting of pale or darker green leaves, because it is still late winter or perhaps earliest spring, is sheer delight. Then there are almonds—*Prunus amygdalo-persica pollardii*, the finest variety, is a cloud of pale pink in March, soft enough to tone beautifully with yellow forsythia like the colours in some Chinese paintings, should they find themselves neighbours, and there are flowering peaches, bushes of rose-pink, which must be carefully placed, for their colour is strong enough for them to quarrel should they disagree with their neighbours.

Although some of them come from French nurseries, lilacs (*Syringa*) seem essentially a part of an English spring. Grown rather formally in a lilac walk or grouped, they furnish delightful masses of colour. Their red, mauve, lilac, carmine and purple shades tone beautifully with the deeper pink and red rhododendrons although, if planting them near rhododendrons it must be done with discretion as, while lilacs like an alkaline soil, rhododendrons will not tolerate lime. A bank of standard laburnums, their long pendulous racemes hanging behind and mingling with white lilacs, can be charming. Fine as their flowers are—and surely they are indispensable in any self-respecting garden—it must be admitted that the foliage of lilacs is not decorative and they are better placed to border some side walk where they can be seen when in flower and left afterwards to wear their rather drab summer dress more or less unseen.

## Beauty of form

Some shrubs have intrinsic beauty of form in addition to the culminating beauty of their flowers, and should be planted in prominent places where their unusual quality can be appreciated. Of such shrubs, Japanese maples are some of the loveliest, especially the red-leaved varieties. Japanese maples do not mind a reasonable degree of frost but should be given a sheltered position as they do not like wind or draughts. When planting a glade each tree or shrub or group of trees or shrubs should be given room in which to attain its natural size and shape, and not be crowded amongst others all struggling for light and air. But there are some shrubs, among them most of the varieties of berberis, which, massed in fairly large groups give brilliant displays of colour. In fact a part of the glade could be given to this genus with the happiest results. *Berberis stenophylla*, attaining a height of from 8 to 10 feet, grows into dense masses of dark green arching foliage covered in its season with deep yellow flowers and it makes rich dark backgrounds against which the deciduous kinds show beautifully.

To name a few of the finer varieties, *B. thunbergii*, an attractive bronze-green during summer, becomes a mass of fiery scarlet in autumn, unsurpassed for the brilliance of its autumn colour. *B. wilsonae*, with semi-evergreen foliage, is covered in autumn with the loveliest coral berries and *B*. Comet, attaining a height of about 4 feet, with arching branches covered later with red berries, is a gorgeous sight. Among the evergreen varieties,

*B. verruculosa* with dense glossy dark green leaves, many of which turn dull red in autumn, is one of the finest evergreen shrubs. *B. darwinii*, in spring a mound of glowing orange, is of outstanding merit, as is, too, the more recent introduction *B. linearifolia* Orange King, perhaps the finest of the genus. With their graceful habit, many of them pendulous or semi-pendulous, berberis are some of the easiest shrubs to grow and they can be planted to make some of the loveliest garden scenes, but the strong yellow and orange flowers which some varieties produce will kill pink rhododendrons or indeed any pink flowers that are unfortunate enough to find themselves near them.

### Tolerant cotoneasters

One fact that makes glades of trees and shrubs so interesting is that so many different subjects can find a home in them. Cotoneasters, a number of which are evergreen or semi-evergreen, planted on dry banks or in partial shade, conditions under which many shrubs would not thrive, will be doubly welcome when covered with their scarlet berries, especially when seen against dark conifers in autumn and early winter. Like so many shrubs, cotoneasters, more especially the taller varieties, are much finer in groups than as single specimens.

There are a number of free-growing varieties, some of them, *C. frigidus* and *C. f. vicari*, growing into small trees, and others forming thick dense masses that are so often needed for shelter in both new and older gardens. The cotoneaster is very amenable, thriving well in comparative shade or in a sun-baked corner, where little except the berberis family will deign to flourish. Heavy or light sandy soil come alike to the varieties of this happy-go-lucky adventurer and little does he mind so long as the soil is moderately well drained.

The smaller-foliaged *C. franchetii* makes a more compact bush. Its barrel-shaped berries, plentifully produced in clusters of 10 or thereabouts, are orange-red. The fishbone cotoneaster, *C. horizontalis*, grows well on a north or an east wall, but it is slower to reach its full size than many other kinds, although in time it will grow to 6 or 8 feet in height. The beauty of the plant is the dull red autumnal colouring of the foliage, which it retains well into the autumn, the lower leaves often colouring and falling before the green leaves on the shoots and branches have turned. Its spreading horizontal growth is most attractive and it will cover dry banks where little else will grow, except perhaps for such plants as St John's Wort, *Hypericum calycinum*. There is, too, an especially dainty silver variegated variety which could be very decorative in the larger pockets of a rock garden.

Turning to the cotoneasters of shrubby habit, we find a large number of species, mainly from expeditions to China and the Himalayas, which have found their way into gardens.

13. The formal
paved garden with
pool at Hascombe
Court, Surrey

14. A pool made
from a widened
stream at
Westwoods,
Windlesham,
Surrey

W... of ... R...lf... B...lf..dd... The informal stream showing effective use of Westmorland stone

As a family, cotoneasters are valuable for their brightly coloured fruits, generally bright scarlet, and there are a few varieties with dark plum coloured berries.

The *frigidus* and *salicifolius* groups are perhaps the most decorative in berry; *C. frigidus*, forming a large bush or small tree, is worth growing as single specimens. Its rich green foliage and plentiful clusters of white flowers in early summer are followed by heavy masses of bright red berries as large as peas, sometimes produced in such prodigality as to weigh down the branches. Perhaps unfortunately, it is deciduous, but the closely allied *C. salicifolius* and *C. henryanus* are evergreen and form thick bushes, their spreading branches wreathed in berries well into winter. One of the choicest of this class, *C. lacteus*, introduced from Yunnan in 1913 by George Forrest, has broader and more rounded leaves than *C. salicifolius*; its clusters of red berries are rather late in ripening, consequently hanging on well into winter. It is a useful plant for glade planting or it can be grown effectively on a wall. There are, too, a number of deciduous specimens of strong growth forming in a few years bushes 6 feet or more in height. With dark green foliage *C. bullatus* has prominently veined leaves, and bright red pear-shaped berries, and *C. hupehensis* bears large rounded red berries. These two are among the most distinctive. For the brilliance of its scarlet fruits there are few to rival *C. rotundifolius*, known sometimes as *C. hookeri*, which, with its horizontal growth, has the appearance of a much enlarged *C. horizontalis*. In the pale sunshine of a winter's day these large, oblong, highly coloured berries are more than welcome.

## Selecting varieties

The extent of any glade will to some degree govern the size of the groups of shrubs which fill its borders, but it is better to have fewer and larger groups than to have a greater number of varieties with the consequent crowded and rather confused result. The object in planting should be to select the finest varieties of any particular genus and to group them in the most effective way. Variety and contrast of form and of colour, both of foliage and of flowers, should be achieved in glade borders. And to this end an occasional group of silver birches, it may be in the borders, it may be in the lawn, could be planted. This apparently accidental but in reality very careful placing of trees can do so much to give gardens the final touches of artistry.

When I am planting glades, the trees and shrubs are put into their allotted places by gardeners from planting plans which are carefully prepared in my office and which show accurately and to scale the exact position of each separate tree or shrub or group of trees or shrubs. It is impossible for me, when visiting gardens I am making, to see every shrub into its exact position, but I like to go later and give what I think of as finishing touches. That is, I may alter the place of some tree or shrub so that it is seen in all its beauty. It may be only to bring a shrub forward here or to make another stand by itself where formerly it was partly hidden by its neighbours; such finishing touches can make a surprising difference.

But to return to the choice of subjects; *Fothergilla major* and *F. monticola*, growing to a height of from 5 to 6 feet, will do well in light shade; *F. monticola* particularly is well worth planting for its wonderful autumn colour. Then there are hamamelis, among the earliest of shrubs to flower and very welcome as harbingers of spring, but decorative as they are when flowering, hamamelis should not be in too prominent a place as their foliage in summer is nothing to boast of. A group of laburnums with their long pendulous racemes can be lovely in flower and an unusual effect can be obtained if bushes are planted in front of taller standard trees, thus making long handsome yellow curtains of flowers. *Laburnum vossii* is the finest variety but it must not be near pink rhododendrons or other shrubs with pink flowers. Laburnums are, however, entirely happy with the bronze shades of *Berberis thunbergii* or indeed with most of the varieties of berberis or with shrubs with white flowers. I have planted laburnums behind *Viburnum tomentosum mariesii* with charming results but perhaps they are seen at their best in an entirely green setting, that is if there are enough of them.

To come unexpectedly on to a group of tree paeonies in some sheltered spot is sheer delight. It must be admitted that the flowering period of these distinctive shrubs is short but their decorative compound foliage is in itself reason enough to entitle them to a place of honour and their flowers are glorious. Among the finer varieties *Paeonia delavayi* has deep crimson flowers followed by large black-seeded fruits, *P. lemoinei* Alice Harding has double flowers, a lovely shade of canary yellow, and *P. lemoinei* Souvenir de Maxime Cornu has very large deep yellow flowers. Again with yellow flowers *P. lutea* is rather smaller, while *P. suffruticosa* is a magnificent shrub, with white, purple, crimson and pink flowers.

Making a small tree, rather like a fairly large bush apple, *Parrotia persica*, a member of the witch-hazel family, should be given plenty of room in which to show its wonderful coloured foliage, which turns crimson and gold early in the autumn and persists for a long time.

## Ornamental cherries

As well as the flowers of cherries, how lovely are the delicate tones of their spring foliage. There are too many varieties to name them separately but *Prunus avium flore pleno*, the double gean, is equally right in park or garden, and *P. hillieri* Spire, finest in groups of say three or more when its slender columns, like Lombardy poplars, only not so tall, give such an effective contrast to round-headed trees or shrubs. If I had to choose one variety of cherry my choice would be a white one, *P.* Tai-Haku; with its large flowers it is supremely lovely. With thinly disposed branches, *Prunus subhirtella autumnalis* flowers intermittently through the winter, reminding us that spring is coming.

Most ornamental cherries, especially the Japanese varieties, can be planted singly or in groups, either as bushes or standards, but most of them are free-growing and should have plenty of room in which to show their distinctive habits. Cheal's Weeping, *P. serrulata rosea*, with its graceful habit, would appear even finer if planted on a slight eminence rather than on level ground. Upright in growth and with bronze young foliage *P. sargentii* is one of the best for autumn colour, and *P.* Hokusai with large double flowers, clear rose-pink opening to pale blush in late April or May, is another tall-growing variety. Although a favourite for street planting, *P.* Kanzan has some shade of magenta in its flowers and if included needs to be carefully placed. The arching branches of *P. yedoensis* become covered with pale pink buds opening to almost white flowers and *P.* Ukon with a spreading habit, has pale lemon-buff, semi-double flowers which go beautifully with its bronze opening foliage. If space allows, cherries in groups of three or more, each group of one variety only, are finer than if planted singly, but to do this does need more room. Becoming a large tree, *P. padus watereri* is lovely as a specimen either in park or garden.

An avenue or walk of prunus in one or more varieties can, in its informal formality, be lovely especially while the cherries are flowering. Such an avenue could be planted with one variety only, or if more varieties are included it would be of greater interest horticulturally. Under the cherries the turf could be planted with stretches of white or white and purple crocus, well to the front. Yellow and white crocus are always good, separately or intermingling, but yellow and purple are not so happy together. Any shades of yellow narcissi could be planted under white-flowered prunus but the paler narcissi are more pleasing than the deeper ones. Tulips, however, go better with pink-flowered prunus than narcissi. Pink, mauve, purple or blood-red tulips would be charming with any white or pink prunus, or with *Prunus* Ukon, the pale lemon-yellow flowers of which against its copper foliage are so distinctive. And the tulips can be naturalised for, if given several applications of weak liquid manure after flowering, they will continue to flower for some years. And imagine how lovely cherries, their branches hanging over drifts of say, the pink tulip Clara Butt, or the blood-red tulip King Harold, would be. Here and there the long pendant racemes of low standard wisterias would make the scene even more beautiful.

Magnolias could be planted with prunus or by themselves. Against a background of *Chamaecyparis lawsoniana allumii* or the darker, stronger-growing *C.* Triomphe de Boskoop, their cup-shaped white or purple-stained flowers would show in all their distinctive beauty. Magnolias are one of the few shrubs that may be grown happily as specimens in a lawn, where there would be nothing to lessen the effect of their almost architectural character. Having enormous flowers, *M. grandiflora* is best grown against a wall, except in the southern counties where it will succeed as a bush. This variety has the estimable quality of being evergreen.

A single plant of *Spiraea arguta* is nothing much to look at but a group of six or more will be striking, in flower a cloud of dainty white lace. *Holodiscus discolor ariaefolius*, sometimes known as *Spiraea ariaefolia*, growing to a height of 10 feet, with large drooping panicles of creamy-white flowers at the tips of its long stems, is distinctive and it flowers in summer. Another fine type is *Spiraea prunifolia flore pleno* with double white flowers wreathing its branches, the foliage of which assumes rich autumn tints.

Later in the year, to come on to a group of pyracanthas glowing with red, orange or yellow berries against a dark background could console us with their fiery splendour for the fact that autumn is coming. Having narrow leaves, grey underneath, *P. angustifolia* is covered with clusters of orange berries; *P. coccinea lalandii* has large orange-red berries; *P. atalantioides* produces large, reddish-orange berries; and *P. rogersiana flava*, a shrub of looser habit, is a yellow-berried type.

The genus *Viburnum* includes several varieties well worth inclusion in any collection of flowering trees and shrubs. Although without any particular merit as to its foliage or shape *V. carlesii* should be grown for its delightful fragrance. A rather slow-growing winter-flowering evergreen, *V. tinus* is worth cultivating for its white, pink-tinted flowers; Clyne Castle is an improved form. Of deciduous varieties *V. burkwoodii* with pink buds opening to large fragrant white flowers grows into a fair sized bush 5 to 6 feet high; it is finer on a wall than when grown in the open.

The genus *Weigela* has several hardy and attractive varieties, amongst which Abel Carrière, deep rose, Bristol Ruby, Conquete and Newport Red, covered with bright red flowers, are all perfectly hardy and well worth a place in glade borders. And the genus *Deutzia*, too, includes several excellent kinds, amongst which Contrast has large mauve-pink flowers with an outer band of purple; Magician has large pink flowers edged with white; *D. longifolia veitchii* has large clusters of deep pink flowers; *D. rosea* is a dwarfer variety, also with rose-pink flowers; these, together with *D. rosea campanulata* with white flowers would, as the various members of a particular genus usually do, make attractive and interesting groups.

A tree heath, *Erica arborea alpina*, with grey-white flowers and fresh green feathery foliage, is worth inclusion for the way in which its flowers tone so beautifully with any colours near them. It is charming with pink or red flowering rhododendrons, but should have a fairly sheltered position.

Rhododendrons are in a class apart. The greater number of the rather taller varieties are evergreen and their flowering season is a long one. One of the earliest to open its crimson flowers, so welcome after winter's scarcity, is *R. nobleanum*, flowering from January to March. Rhododendrons really belong to the fringes of woodland and like the intermittent

16. The formal water garden at Westfields, Bedfordshire

17. A small garden glade, its curving borders planted with flowering trees and shrubs, at the Old Parsonage, Marlow, Buckinghamshire

18. A rhododendron glade shaded by oaks at Busbridge Wood, Surrey

19. The garden glade at Westfields, Bedfordshire, with flowering shrubs and trees

shade of oaks (Plate 18). With here and there a few silver birches, and an occasional fir or cypress planted well forward amongst them to diversify their outline, a rhododendron glade can be at the same time supremely lovely and yet a very natural part of a garden. Perhaps no shrub has had so many new introductions of sterling merit as this genus. Their flowering season is a long one, from January to July.

Camellias, too, are evergreen and in favourable localities will bloom from December to April, and even if frosted they will produce flowers from latent buds. Among the aristocrats of plants, camellias are worth a place to themselves, or, in a sheltered position, one or more groups would add very much to the interest of any glade of trees and shrubs.

## Summer flowering shrubs

As so many of them flower in spring and early summer, shrubs that flower later in the year should, when conditions are suitable, be included in every glade of trees and shrubs. The lavender and purple shades of buddleias flowering in July and August, perhaps rather sombre in themselves, look so much more effective when seen against pink or crimson flowers. The pendulous branches of *Buddleia alternifolia* covered with rosy-mauve blooms next to pink escallonias would be a charming harmony of colour. To show its graceful habit *B. alternifolia* should be allowed to grow tall or be planted on a low bank or on a slight eminence.

Quite unlike other members of the broom family both in its thick racemes of flowers and its grey leaves, *Cytisus battandieri* is scented and should be given a fairly sheltered place. Then there is *Spartium junceum*, its rush-like stems covered with deliciously scented flowers, a deep yellow yet without any trace of harshness, from July onwards.

Philadelphus, too, flowering in June and July and in colder districts well into August, may be classed amongst summer-flowering shrubs. Most of the varieties of this genus are scented and, properly pruned, are very beautiful. The aim in pruning should be to have their long branches growing separately, when they will be covered with flowers for their entire length. Among the finer varieties are *P*. Beauclerk, vigorous in growth with strongly scented flowers flushed with pink at the base of thick broad petals; *P*. Belle Etoile, whose single white flowers have a maroon blotch at the base of the petals; *P. grandiflorus* with large single flowers—this species pays for its size by being scentless; and *P. coronarius*, well worth planting for its rich fragrance.

In sunlight the foliage of *Cotinus coggygria foliis purpureis* is a wonderful colour, a rich deep crimson, and its light purple, lace-like inflorescence adds so much to its beauty. It is at its best behind lower growing shrubs with yellow flowers; the floribunda rose Allgold, or indeed any floribunda rose with clear yellow or red flowers, would be an effective contrast. Hypericums, too, would be equally good, but the foliage of this cotinus would tone beautifully with any clear colours except perhaps some shades of pink. I once had a large semicircle, the climax to a long stretch of lawn, planted with this shrub and in front of it, again a complete semi-circle, several rows of scarlet, orange and amber dahlias. The result was a magnificent blaze of colour.

Hydrangeas, particularly near the sea, will flower for a long time. Even their dead flower heads are decorative and should be left on the plants as protection until the following spring. Useful as they are for growing in boxes and tubs, hydrangeas are at their best massed in borders by themselves and the more there are the better they will look.

Several varieties of euonymus, the spindle tree, should be included. Their flowers are nothing much but their fruits, looking as if the whole plant were covered with flowers during late summer and autumn, are striking. Good kinds to grow are *E. yedoensis* with pinkish-purple fruits, a colour as difficult to describe as it is effective; *E. europaeus* producing brilliant red fruits; and *E. alatus* with corky bark, all with richly coloured good autumn foliage.

For a southern aspect *Romneya coulteri*, the Californian poppy, has white flowers with the loveliest golden yellow centres against its very grey cut leaves. Ceanothus and *R. coulteri* together make a delicately lovely colour harmony. There is, too, *Genista aetnensis*, the Mount Etna broom, a large shrub or small tree with pendulous growth which produces its yellow flowers in July; it looks its best in a setting of green foliage.

Another useful although not spectacular genus of shrubs is potentilla. The flowers are in shades of yellow and white and continue to appear throughout summer and autumn. Their feathery foliage can be a pleasing change from that of shrubs with heavier foliage and *P. fruticosa vilmoriniana* with silvery leaves and cream flowers will tone with flowers of almost any colour.

Forest trees and conifers take a long time to attain maturity but many shrubs and small flowering trees grow quickly. To obtain the appearance of a well-furnished garden in a comparatively short time, if, say, silver birches are planted here and there in the borders, they will give a mature appearance almost from the time of planting. Those subjects that form the permanent planting should, to avoid the need for rearrangement, be at their correct distances.

Dwarf varieties of berberis, potentillas, *Cytisus praecox* and other low-growing shrubs, which should be planted in groups, are labour saving because they grow into dense masses through which weeds find it difficult to penetrate. *Juniperus chinensis pfitzeriana* and *J. sabina tamariscifolia*, too, from their density effectively discourage weeds.

A few groups of the strong-growing, later flowering herbaceous plants in bold groups amongst the shrubs and in carefully chosen places would give colour later in the year. Groups of delphiniums, kniphofias, heliopsis, heleniums and colonies of the later flowering hardy lilies, would gain in beauty from their informal green setting.

# {❧ 5 ❧}

# *Japanese Gardens*

FROM ITALY we have learnt how to use ornaments, sculpture and statuary to enrich our own gardens. From France we have learnt to make elaborate formal gardens, perhaps more with trees than with flowers, but from Japan we can learn from a totally different kind of design. It is doubtful if a Japanese garden which conforms strictly to the Japanese tradition would find much favour in Great Britain, but if we can catch the spirit of Japanese design, the artistry with which the various stones, plants and any other materials are used in its making, and above all the excellent feeling of balance that is obtained by their skilful use, then we can make something that is as unusual as it is beautiful.

Japanese gardens may be formal or informal, or they may be both in the same garden. But whether formal or informal, these gardens should show a perfection of balance in the placing of every stone, plant, tree or shrub that goes to their making.

## *Symbolism in design*

In the greater number of Japanese gardens there is water; it may be a stream, it may be that an existing spring or pool can be used, but in whatever form water is present it must fit happily into the scheme as a whole. A level site could well be used for a more formal type of garden, although the word formal would not, I imagine, have the same meaning in Japan as in this country. Symbolism enters to a very considerable degree into the design of those Japanese gardens that are true to historical tradition, but as this book is concerned more with their influence on English gardens than with the tradition or history of Japanese gardens we need consider tradition only so far as we can learn from it in making our own gardens.

And in this connection we have much to learn. Gardens of Nippon are classified generally into two types, flat or hillside gardens. As the name *tsukiyama*—artificial hills—suggests, such gardens consist of a hill or hills, and a stream or pools. *Hira-nawa*, level gardens, are perhaps the nearest to our own so-called formal gardens. There is, however, a marked

59

difference between the two, but the Japanese feeling for balance is always apparent, even in formal gardens. This inherent love of balance appears in many and various ways. The boundaries may be regular or irregular, there may be stones, carefully chosen for their size and shape, placed to retain rising soil, but always where they tell to the greatest advantage in the garden as a whole and placed with due regard to their natural stratification. There may be a bed or beds, probably circular, but with their edges pleasingly broken with more stones. And it is this quality of balanced informality that makes Japanese gardens so interesting to plan.

To design and make this kind of informal garden is something like painting a picture. Plants, trees and shrubs must not be too large, for one tree or shrub that is so large as to be out of scale could lessen the aesthetic value of the whole garden. Such a garden, really a landscape in miniature, is particularly suitable for the often necessarily smaller gardens of today.

## Proportion and balance

To achieve success, first it is necessary to make a plan to scale. This plan should show the exact size and shape of the ground to be dealt with. It should show any trees, water if there is water, and any other existing features. It should, too, show any difference of levels. The qualities to aim at are good proportions and perfect balance in the placing of trees, shrubs, rocks or indeed of any materials. Light and shade, too, must be carefully considered. These last attributes include the shadows cast, say, by an overhanging stone on to water, or some branch—it may be from a twisted pine. If it is possible to obtain a dwarf, misshapen pine or conifer this could be planted where it would become a focal point to which near planting should be made subservient.

## Suitable shrubs

Some shrubs that are suitable for inclusion in a garden of this sort are *Juniperus sabina tamariscifolia*, which forms attractive low mounds of greyish-green foliage, and there is, too, the freer growing *J. chinensis pfitzeriana*, a lovely spreading evergreen. There are Japanese maples in shades of bronze, red, yellow and green. With finely cut foliage *Acer palmatum dissectum atropurpureum* is one of the loveliest both for its habit and for its colour. It is deciduous but, crimson all the summer, it takes on even richer autumn colouring and its bare dense mass of branches is charming even without leaves. Green during the summer, *A.* Osakazuki is perhaps the finest for autumn colour.

When possible some slight hollow should be chosen as the site for a Japanese garden,

20. This woodland glade points the contrast with the garden glade shown in Plate 19.

21. Garden of
Tenryuji Temple,
Kyoto

22. Garden of
Katsura Villa,
Kyoto

and it does not matter how much the ground twists and turns. To go round a corner and to come upon something, a spreading pine or juniper or a Japanese maple growing over a moss-grown boulder, would be a picture in itself. And such a garden should be a series of pictures, each lovely and yet differing from its neighbours, a constantly changing panorama so that one would wish to stop and look at each unfolding scene. It should always be remembered, when making such a garden that one is using Japanese influence in what will really be an English garden, not trying to follow the rules that govern the making of traditional Japanese gardens. And this is because we like more spacious gardens as against the rather narrow walks and paths that are suitable for the Japanese whose physique is generally smaller than our own.

## Background plants

A Japanese garden should be a separate unit in the general scheme and, having decided its boundaries, suitable trees or shrubs should be planted as backgrounds. The greyish-green foliage of *Pinus mugo* is so natural in appearance and it can be kept to any desired height by judicious cutting back. Variable in habit, *Juniperus chinensis pfitzeriana* may grow into a rather flat, even shape but usually its branches make separate layers with dark shadows between their horizontal growths. This contrast of light and shade, which can be emphasised by cutting away the drooping growths which hang from the upper branches, makes the mature plant particularly lovely. It should never be trimmed into the shape of a hedge, its beauty lies in its natural habit of growth and in the pleasing grey-green of its foliage. If this conifer, growing to a height of from 5 to 6 feet, is not high enough to give the necessary feeling of enclosure, Japanese cherries would be charming behind it, particularly if rather low weeping varieties were chosen, but the cherries should be far enough back so that their branches do not overhang the junipers. The upright members of the juniper family, too, are some of the most distinctive of evergreens and could be used to diversify the backgrounds, especially if planted in groups. Almost any colours look well against the glaucus foliage of *J. virginiana*—one of the hardiest. The Chinese juniper, *J. chinensis*, is a close-growing columnar form with a slightly brownish tint in its foliage. With its upward turning habit of growth it is, when mature, a conifer of unusual character, but it should not be used with pink flowers.

It is well worth while to plant enough evergreens as backgrounds as the tracery of many bare deciduous branches is so lovely against them, and, depending as it does so much on form, a Japanese garden is a garden for winter as well as summer.

As well as their flowers, the arching branches of some species of roses are so graceful even when not in flower that they, too, would form effective backgrounds. A suitable type is *Rosa hugonis* with soft yellow flowers that tone with any colours; *R.* Frühlingsgold is another with fine sprays of yellow flowers, but without quite the attractive arching habit of *R. hugonis*, and there are many others.

## A matter of form

Because form is so all-important in a Japanese garden, one should choose trees and shrubs for their form rather than for their flowers and, having chosen them, they must be so placed that their unusual shapes can be seen and enjoyed to the full. A Japanese maple, a twisted pine, a low-growing juniper, in fact almost any shrub that has unusual character, could stand alone rising from a carpet of, say, *Veronica incana* or *Juniperus procumbens* or low-growing ericas; *Calluna vulgaris hammondii* is excellent for this purpose, as indeed are any of the dwarf heaths; and if cut hard back each year will grow into a dense carpet of dark green, the richest setting for lilies.

No flowers could be lovelier or more distinctive than the white trumpets of *Lilium regale* with nothing near them to detract from their purity of form and colour. If colour is needed, the orange flowers of *L. tigrinum* would gain immensely from the dark carpet beneath them. The varieties of *L. umbellatum*, too, would be equally effective. To make such a garden will give lasting pleasure for, like collecting pictures or other works of art, one may add from time to time new or interesting shrubs or plants with the subsequent delight of placing them where they reveal all their beauty.

## An imaginary garden

To take an imaginary walk through an embryo garden, we enter the lawn which sweeps through it. It must have a turf carpet, for with gravel much of its charm would be lost. On one side a Japanese maple, lovely alike in shape and its rich shade of foliage red, grows over a massive boulder almost on to the turf. Farther away on the opposite side a dwarf pine spreads horizontally over another stone with a carpet of bright blue *Veronica* True Blue, to be repeated still farther down the length of the garden on the opposite side so that the nicest feeling of balance is maintained. Close to the stream and with their roots in the damp soil, *Iris kaempferi*, those aristocrats of the iris family, lift their distinctive flat blooms in lovely shades of mauve, and purple that is almost black and there are others, some with white flowers. There are hostas, with chaste flowers above grey-green foliage with more lilies growing taller behind them. Their glaucous leaves are the best foil for white lilies and equally good with yellow or orange. Both with pale lilac flowers, *Hosta fortunei* and *H. sieboldiana* are good for their glaucous colouring. We go on and come to a group of *Chamaecyparis lawsoniana wisselii* with its characteristic ragged dark green foliage.

To balance this farther down on the opposite side, a group of Irish junipers stand erect and columnar with grey-green feathery foliage, rising sentinel-like from a carpet of *Penstemon heterophyllus*, its flowers a lovely shade of soft blue. To walk through this garden is something like walking through an alpine valley in miniature. Turning one corner one is irresistibly drawn on to see what will unfold itself round the next.

There is a group of Kurume azaleas, their colours gorgeous when in flower and their close foliage forming cushions of dense evergreen. Lilies again are lovely with these evergreen azaleas, only there should be enough of them to give telling groups. On seeing the garden a horticulturally-minded Japanese might say that he had never seen anything like it in Japan but, if truthful, he would add that it was very beautiful.

## Ornaments

These enter largely into the making of Japanese gardens: bridges, lamps, lanterns and *torii*. When there are islands bridges would form the means of getting from the garden mainland to the island or when, as was sometimes the case in the older Japanese gardens, a dry watercourse was made to simulate the course of a non-existent stream, a bridge might be built to add to the effect as well as to afford a means of getting from one side to the other. Lawns did not form a part of the older types of Japanese gardens and the soil near a stream or pool was trodden and kept damp by watering. In some gardens the soil might be covered with white sand, the sand being raked into ornamental patterns. This would scarcely be possible today because of the time it would take—a lawn would be both more permanent and more pleasing.

Lamps or stone lanterns, the lanterns admittedly more decorative than useful, figure largely in traditional Japanese gardens. Now they are seldom if ever used for lighting but probably, from their symbolic signs, they had religious significance. *Torii*, too, were traditionally often used as ornaments. A *torii* consists of two upright wooden posts connected at the top by two cross timbers, the lower of the two straight and the upper curved upwards at each end. They were introduced into gardens from Shinto temples but their religious significance, I believe, has never been explained.

## Rock gardens

Japanese gardens should not be confused with rock gardens. The two are entirely different, for whereas Japanese gardens, apart from their tradition, depend very much upon form and balance for their effect, rock gardens give opportunities for masses of early colour and for growing a variety of interesting plants that could not suitably be grown in other parts of the garden. But this is not to say that due attention should not be given to form in rock gardens. When constructing a rock garden every attention should be paid to the stratification of the rocks, that is, each stone should be laid on its natural bed and the courses, the layers of stone of which the garden is made, should give an orderly feeling of line. The stones, for stability and to guide rain water to the plants, should be laid with a slight slope inwards, that is to the plant pockets.

23. The lake at The Aviary, Southall

24. Another view of The Aviary, Southall, showing the lawn and glade bordering the lake

25. Nepeta, roses and delphiniums lining the lower terrace at Ardleigh, Chigwell, Essex

26. A small formal garden at Frognal, London

27. Old Hall Cottage,
Frinton-on-Sea.
Lawn with rose
garden and
herbaceous borders

28. Formal garden
with silver birches
at The Cottage,
Le Touquet

# 6

# *Aspects of Design*

## WATER AS A PRINCIPAL FEATURE
### *Plates 23, 24*

THE LAKE is the principal feature in the grounds of The Aviary, Southall. So close to London, surrounded by woodlands bordering the extensive sheet of water, the garden might be miles away from any town. The house on its principal garden front opens on to a paved terrace from which a lawn descends in an easy slope to the lake. Across the lake another lawn goes to a long stone seat which, standing against a background of tall cypresses, is an effective termination to the vista from the house.

Although the garden contains many fine trees and shrubs it is the stretch of water, glistening, shining in sunlight, reflecting the colours of rhododendrons and the varying shades of green on its banks, that is the centre of all the surrounding loveliness. Although weeping willows, *Salix babylonica*, can be grown under drier conditions, their long pendulous growths never look so well as when hanging over water. Willows grow into large trees and the lake at The Aviary is extensive enough for them to be seen in all their beauty. Walking through the woods one comes to the lawn fringed with rhododendrons, with the house facing us in the distance. But instead of going down the slope to the lake which, to get to the house one must either swim, or row across in a boat which is not always there, one follows a path leading to the bridge at the western end.

From the centre of the bridge one sees the finest view. On the water there are many ducks swimming like tiny live boats, busy in a placid sort of way in feeding themselves; there are, too, Chinese and other special kinds of geese and black swans, floating shapes of loveliness, adding a final distinctive note. This picture, framed between the varying foliage of the trees that line the banks on either side, is like a Corot painting, only alive with constantly changing interest.

In the woods there are avenues of ornamental cherries, lovely when in flower and later there is the colour of their autumn foliage; there are rowans laden in early autumn with clusters of scarlet berries; there are silver birches. There are several groups of the 'Lombardy poplar' cherry, *Prunus* Amanogawa, from seven to a dozen in a group, their columnar growths contrasting so effectively with the lower round-headed trees. Clumps of Lombardy poplars, too, growing high above their neighbours, all help to make the landscape attractive.

### Formal contrast

If only as a contrast to the informality of the glades some formal treatment was necessary. The gardens are, however, bounded on the east by a lofty brick wall. This wall, under which a wide border is planted with peonies and Michaelmas daisies, shelters the western end of the gardens and here a formal rose garden was made. This garden, in full view from the windows and terrace, gives the necessary colour, but as the wild-fowl are not good gardeners, and take an unwelcome interest in the roses, the beds have to be protected from their depredations by wire netting guards which, it must be admitted, slightly detract from the appearance of the rose garden. However, for this there is the compensation of life in its many activities.

## A GARDEN ON TWO LEVELS
### Plate 26

That it was possible to make this garden at Frognal in London on two levels adds very much to its interest. The garden is small and enclosed by brick walls and buildings. It had to be formal.

There is a terrace on to which french windows open on the southern side of the house. From here steps lead down to the sunken lawn which is surrounded by flower borders in which delphiniums, shasta daisies, hemerocallis and phlox form a permanent background to the tulips and narcissi which flower early. Opposite the french windows and steps, just where it is most effective, water spouts from a lion's head on the wall into a pool.

The shallow stone steps, the width of the lawn, give breadth and an illusion of greater space than would a low retaining wall. The beds on the higher level are planted with roses, growing behind them azaleas, *Lilium testaceum* and the handsome later-flowering *L. auratum*. The garden is a setting in character with the pleasant Georgian house.

## TERRACES ON SLOPING GROUND
*Plate 25*

The ground at Ardleigh, Chigwell, Essex, slopes steeply from the principal garden front to the southern boundary. On the steep gradient brick walls are built to support the terraces. The walls, a comfortable sitting height above the paving, enable one to enjoy the colours and fragrance of the garden below.

The upper terrace, which extends for the length of the house on its southern elevation, has large tubs filled with tulips, to be followed by ivy-leaved geraniums for the summer. And here may I say that, while in spring it does not really matter how vivid the colours of tulips and narcissi on terraces are, in summer colours should be softer or there is a risk of their clashing with, or at any rate lessening the value of the colours in the more distant flower borders. Scarlet geraniums in the foreground as an instance, could ruin the appearance of borders that are predominantly pink in their colour scheme. The colours on the terrace should be a harmonious introduction to the more distant flowers that are seen with them.

Roses, with delphiniums behind them, make the lower terrace a rose walk and the bright lavender-blue flowers of *Nepeta faassenii* increase the feeling of formality in a charming way. To plant *N. faassenii* as an edging is as right in this straight paved walk as it would be wrong planted to edge the borders that flank the glade lawn. The glade, so complete a contrast to the formal terraces, extends from the upper north-eastern part of the garden, to end in a little stream in which water falls in several rock-bound pools.

In the glade borders there are philadelphus, *Cytisus albus*, its white flowers charming among pink rhododendrons, lilacs in purples and vinous red, *Rosa moyesii*, an effective splash of blood-red, and *R. hugonis*, its curving branches wreathed in soft yellow flowers. Yellow heleniums, tall sunflowers and Michaelmas daisies and groups of dahlias, dwarf varieties in front with taller growing varieties behind them, prolong the flowering season well into the autumn. Commencing with narcissi and tulips there is colour in these borders from spring until autumn frosts end the floral year.

## CURVING LINES CREATING AN ILLUSION OF SPACE
*Plate 27*

In the lawn on the entrance front at Old Hall Cottage, Frinton-on-Sea, there were three elms, old trees in a row but standing well apart. They chequered the lawn with light and shade and gave character and a feeling of age to the entrance front. At the back the tiled roof of Frinton Old Church, visible above the lower shrubs, added a picturesque note. Other than these, the site had nothing of particular interest. It is a comparatively small garden and it was my intention to make it appear as large as possible. To do this is very much a matter of right proportions, for with the skilful use of curving lines and by keeping everything to scale, almost any garden can be made to appear larger than it is.

The house stands close to the southern boundary of the garden. From the entrance the lawn sweeps under the high elms, curves to the right, past the rose garden and on to the terrace and the western boundary. Walking round from the front the scene unfolds like some moving picture. Brick piers, enclosing the curve of the rose garden, are balanced by the curving outer borders. Between the rose garden on one side and the opposite borders the lawn sweeps, a green carpet, forming the nicest setting for the colours in the borders. Nature was in her kindest mood when she gave us the varied shades of green in all their richness as a kind of backcloth to the colours of shrubs and flowers.

Facing us, as we round the curve of the glade on the western boundary, is a herbaceous border, a climax of colour to which the lawn with its curving borders of shrubs, leads.

Although fairly close to the sea the garden is sheltered by the shrubs and trees growing in the churchyard and in adjacent ground; and, in small gardens, the best place to have trees is beyond the garden boundaries. The trees can be such excellent backgrounds and, if far enough away, there is no drip from their branches and their roots do not rob the soil of nourishment.

When making a new garden next in importance to the design comes the placing of the larger trees and shrubs. In this garden they were carefully chosen for their decorative value and they were equally carefully placed. As one enters, a border on the right, filled with varieties of mop-head hydrangeas, is a long bank of rich pinks, blues, crimson and purples from mid-summer onwards. Hydrangeas need little attention, only a light pruning once a year to keep straggly growth tidy, but they do need copious supplies of water in dry weather.

## FORMAL FEATURES IN AN INFORMAL SETTING
### *Plate 28*

A long panel of lawn extends from The Cottage, Le Touquet, to the boundary. Flagstones, which were laid to border this lawn on each side, give it an attractive formality, to which the silvery trunks of old birches left standing in the lawn add a picturesque note. To one side the lawn leads into a glade of flowering trees and shrubs and on the opposite side into yet another lawn, at the far end of which there is the colour of the roses in a paved rose garden.

With the birches and pines, the long formal flower walk, the rose garden and its spreading lawns, the gardens merge into their setting of trees so that one is scarcely conscious of any boundaries.

## RHYTHMIC CURVES
*Plates 29, 30*

Curving steps on the garden front of this house at Woodford, Essex, go down to a lawn which extends to the limit of the garden. The curve of the steps is answered by a curving mass of rhododendrons in the bed farther down on the opposite side, a harmonious rhythm of curves which is continued by more curving groups of shrubs to the bottom of the garden. It is a small garden but the rhythmic treatment of softly curving steps and borders creates an illusion of greater size than would have been given by a more formal treatment.

## PROTECTION IN A SEASIDE GARDEN
*Plates 31, 32*

There is nothing between the garden at The White House, Sandwich Bay, and the sea but a stretch of sandy foreshore. In designing and planting the garden salt-laden spray had to be taken into consideration, and also wind, risk of drought and the light sandy soil. Nothing would grow higher than a foot or so above the wall on the southern, the exposed, side. At this height plant growth was cut level as though with a knife. To make a garden under such conditions was something of a challenge.

### Nucleus of the garden

The really very straightforward design is for a sunken centre part with surrounding walks and borders on a higher level, the whole enclosed by the outer boundary walls. In the lowest part and central on a principal window a lily pool forms the nucleus round which the garden is created.

Shelter from the salt-laden winds was essential if plants were to grow happily and it is provided mainly in two ways—by sinking the garden, especially the centre part, to as great a depth as was proportionately right, and by the enclosing walls. Entrance from the road is through a wrought iron gate, but decorative as wrought iron gates can be, they do let in wind and draughts and, to obviate this and at the same time to retain their decorative quality, the gates are closely fitted with transparent plastic coverings.

The walls of the rectangular forecourt are covered with vines, honeysuckles, ampelopsis and jasmine. A paved walk leads from the gate to the front door. The court is, in its treatment, formal, with flower borders against the walls and a central panel of lawn, unbroken except for the flagstones of the path which extends from the gate to the door, and the path parallel with the house to a gate, the entrance to the main garden.

## Interest within the gardens

Entirely self-contained and with no vistas on to scenery beyond their boundary walls, interest had to be created within the gardens. The difference in levels, together with the varying character of the planting in the pool garden and the outer walks, all helped to make the garden interesting. Choice of plants had to be confined to subjects that would stand the salt-laden spray, but when one comes to use them, there is a surprising number that will thrive under such conditions. Most plants with grey foliage will grow well near the sea and *Phlomis fruticosa* and *Senecio laxifolius* have become great mounds of grey foliage, studded in their flowering season with countless numbers of yellow flowers. Iris, too, thrive in the rather dry soil. Lavender—old English, Munstead and the deep purple Hidcote —seems to appear in vacant spaces over the whole garden. Only there are no vacant spaces because the owner has added a number of interesting foliage and other plants.

Standing on the terrace and looking down the length of the garden there are steps to a sunken pool garden. Paving surrounds the pool, which has in its centre a charming fountain figure. Although I do not propose to give in detail the plants, one notices the luxuriance of the planting. Flanking the southern walk on the higher level, banks of mop-head hydrangeas, *H. paniculata grandiflora* and *H. sargentiana* flourish, their flowers lasting a long time. There are good groups of floribunda and species roses, the latter throwing long arching growths. There are *Berberis thunbergii*, *B. wilsonae* and *B. rubrostilla* for their summer and autumn colours with, as a foil to their resplendent masses, the rich bronze-green of *B. verruculosa*.

Steps at the far end of the pool garden lead up to the outer turf walk which gives the opportunity for growing many plants in groups large enough for them to be seen at their finest in the general scheme. On the northern side the curve of low swelling hills not only gives additional protection, it seems to be a part of, and certainly adds to the beauty of the garden. But it is the wealth of flowers and the luxuriance of growth that strikes one in the garden at The White House.

## A SENSE OF STABILITY

*Plates 33, 34, 35, 36*

Built in 1914, when the original garden was laid out, Hungerdown House is in the Georgian tradition. The site occupies a sloping shelf overlooking the upper valley of the Bristol Avon, and enjoys a wide view—which takes the visitor by surprise as he first steps on to the terrace—to east and south, over typical grassland country.

The architectural character of a country house, such as this, demands a certain amount of formality in its immediate surroundings. An attempt had been made to provide this, but on an inadequate scale, which called for extension if the house was to avoid the appearance of being perched rather insecurely on its slope, giving almost the impression of being in danger of sliding down into the valley.

Formality and the sense of stability on a sloping site alike call for terracing, steps, retaining walls and so on. These features, which must never be forced on a site, can, however, be of great value if they are appropriate to the setting. Ashlar and balustrading are now expensive, but in this case squared Cotswold building stone laid in courses, with yew hedges planted on top, make a not unsatisfactory substitute. A garden on a sloping site will almost inevitably call for greater expense in layout than one on the flat. But there are many compensations.

On the site (see plan on page 20) are two large oaks (A), and the house had been well placed in relation to them. Here the professional eye is apparent, but apart from that placing many opportunities were missed and many things done which should not have been done and cannot now be undone. A more formal approach than that provided through an orchard would be desirable. The large forecourt was left in its original slope, tilting to the front door. To level it now would bring it over the damp course of the house, which is impossible. There are further complications in the levels on the garden side which had to be accepted as they were. In these days of earth shifting machinery the preparation of a site like this no longer presents difficulties and money spent on it is certainly well spent.

Next, continuing my criticism of the work originally done, I come to the point which was obvious to layman and professional alike. The kitchen garden occupied the whole area of the present glade, dominating the garden. Furthermore, the site occupied by vegetables presented an exceptional opportunity to the landscapist. Besides the general slope to the river already mentioned, there is a distinct dip in the ground. Thus in a garden of moderate size were to be found slopes running three ways. I hope the opportunity so presented has not been missed.

## The house surrounds

To give formality to the immediate surroundings of the house it was, in my opinion, necessary to extend the terraced area and in doing so to return the long front lawn round the south side of the house. The natural lie of the land enabled this to be done on three levels, the oak tree providing me with a perfect centre point to their alignment, while the fountain became the pivot of the whole design. This makes a focal point to both vistas and keys the whole design together.

I have already mentioned the generally horizontal effect given by the view. To provide a contrast to this, cypresses were planted in pairs down the length of the long lawn. Besides providing the vertical lines we required these considerably increase the illusion of length. The borders on each side of this lawn were first planted with herbaceous subjects, but now to reduce work, shrubs, chiefly roses—shrub, hybrid musk and floribunda—will be introduced more and more; I hope very much that it will be ultimately possible to edge these borders with stone which would greatly increase the effect of the whole.

Originally there were steps, rough, narrow and steep in tread, leading from the house level to this lawn and then again from it to the lower one. These have been replaced with others of better quality, which are better proportioned in size and width to the house. The tumbled grey-green mass of *Phlomis fruticosa* looks very satisfactory against the clear-cut stone of the lower steps. Its flowers are not altogether easy in colour, but as a small ever-green to associate with stonework it is of the greatest value.

At Hungerdown House the formality of the terraces (B) on the east and south is carried round to a long straight cherry walk (C) which extends for the length of the garden on its north-western boundary. This formal treatment of trees and mown lawn gives a happy transition from formal to informal gardens.

## A pool garden

From the long flower terrace, a flight of steps leads down from its southern end into a circular pool garden (D). This pool garden is important, it is the focal turning point from the long terrace into the gardens, still formal, which lead through the sundial garden into the informal formality of the cherry walk. The pool garden, which is paved with radiating stones and has in its centre a circular pool with a lead figure spouting water into a stone basin, is a focal point between the south and east terraces, to both of which it gives a sense of completion. From the pool garden, two sets of steps rise to a lawn (E) on which the oak already mentioned casts its spreading shade. The tree dominates this lawn and other than paeonies in front with phlox or Michaelmas daisies behind, which fill the side borders, no

29. Informal lawn
bordered by
curving mass of
rhododendrons and
shrubs at
Woodford, London

30. Another view
at Woodford,
showing the
curving steps going
down from the
garden front of the
house

31. The lily pool at The White House, Sandwich Bay

32. The White House, Sandwich; the garden is sunken for protection from wind

33. The lily pool and steps up to one of the two magnificent oaks at Hungerdown House, Wiltshire

34. The glade seen from the upper terrace at Hungerdown

35. Steps on to the lower lawn from the long flower terrace at Hungerdown

36. Formal garden with a wellhead in the centre at Hungerdown

37. The pool garden at the far end of the centre lawn, Hillside, Four Oaks, Warwickshire

38. The highest terrace and the main lawn, with the pool garden in the distance, at Hillside, Four Oaks

39. A long, formal herbaceous walk at Langham Hall, near Colchester

40. The semicircular rotunda at Stonley Woods, Yorkshire

further planting was necessary. It is a quiet interlude from which another flight of steps leads up to the formal sundial garden (F). Originally designed as a rose garden, it has, to save labour, been planted as a formal garden with seats and a centre sundial. There is a dignity in fine ornaments suitably placed and I am not sure that when furnished and given character in this way this garden will not be more distinctive than had its original purpose been fulfilled. But the flowers of the roses will be lacking.

## Cherry tree walk

The flowering season in the cherry walk extends for a full six weeks, from the time when *Prunus yedoensis* and *P. sargentii* start till the last petals fall from *P. albo-rosea* or Shirofugen. Here the central panel of grass is kept mown short while the sides are allowed to grow long. For its length the walk is a little too broad and by this simple device an illusion of greater length is given. The sides, too, being left unmown until midsummer, provide a home for bulbs and corms. Coinciding in its flowering with the majority of the cherries, *Anemone apennina* has been massed on both sides; in time they should make a sheet of blue from end to end.

In our survey of this garden we now find ourselves at the point farthest from the house—at the meeting-point of the glade (G) and cherry walk vistas—and we can now look back at the house and its attendant terraces. The shrub borders accommodate many of the best varieties of the principal lime-tolerant species, so that it can be said that there will be something either in flower, or in full glory of leaf, at every season of the year. But undoubtedly the main effect is that provided by the high summer display of massed shrub roses, delphiniums, cistus and *regale* lilies. Rather than make any more detailed description of the planting I wish to call attention to certain aspects, the full significance of which may not be at once apparent.

## Groups of conifers

A marked feature is the strong group of *Chamaecyparis* Triomphe de Boskoop and *allumii*, backing against the cherry walk at the end nearest the sundial garden. These trees, now approaching 20 feet in height, give substance to the garden throughout the year and by their placing balance the site, for the wide distances on the south side seem to call for something really solid at this point.

Then there are the little groups of birch trees in the mown lawn. Their slender trunks and light foliage make a complete contrast with the dark cypresses and they again play their part throughout the year. At Hungerdown the birches are seen against a background of chamaecyparis and shrubs. They would, however, be equally effective against blue sky

73

or against white walls. For a few trees in a prominent position it pays to hasten the moment when the bark takes on its silver coat by giving them an occasional scrub. Lastly we have four bold groups of *Juniperus chinensis pfitzeriana*, a horizontal growing evergreen to contrast with the vertical lines of the chamaecyparis and the light grace of the birches. I regard groups of this shrub as being of the greatest value in bringing unity to a garden—subject to one point; its proper pruning is essential, for without that it will become a shapeless mass and soon outgrow its allotted position. From time to time whole branches should be removed to make way for younger ones pointing in the same direction and these in their turn will give place to their successors. If the work is done before Christmas an ample supply of evergreen decoration is available.

## CROSS LEVELS
### Plates 11, 37, 38

At Hillside, Four Oaks, Warwicks., the ground slopes high to the west, low to the east, in front of the terrace and the principal windows of the house. There were large heaps of soil in all directions. The problem was how to treat these cross levels. The obvious answer was to terrace the garden and I designed two terraces, a lower glade and a rose garden. The highest terrace, to the west, is a turf walk with flower borders on either side. A flight of steps built in the centre of the walk descends to the main lawn. This lawn, centred on the principal garden front of the house, is wide and level and from it yet more steps descend to the third garden, thus giving a vista across the garden from east to west. As a complete change this, the lowest garden, is made into a glade of trees and shrubs.

Nepeta, purple thymes and campanulas drape a low stone wall built to the west to retain the soil on the highest terrace. Hillside is in a residential area, enclosed on three sides by mature forest trees, but it seems a country garden for the large rhododendrons, moved from a previous garden, and the cupressus merge visually into the background of trees so naturally that its boundaries seem lost in the surrounding woodlands.

*Heightened interest*

But looking from the terrace the picture was not complete. It needed heightened interest. And to give this interest a pool garden was made at the far end of the centre lawn. On its stone pedestal, a lead fountain figure in the pool is a dominant note and it is, too, a focal point from the central vista and the cross vistas leading from the upper walk on the western side of the lawn to the glade on the eastern side.

To the east of the terrace the rose garden is paved, with square or rectangular beds, each filled with one variety only. Enclosing yew hedges make it a separate garden and the stone tubs and bench, together with an ancillary sundial standing high in the centre, give it a richness of design and ornament that is in complete contrast to the informal glade into which it leads. I have been asked if stone seats and ornaments are not out of character in smaller gardens. The answer is no. I have used marble well-heads, stone or marble seats or tables in very small places with the happiest results. There are gardens in which they would not be right. As an instance such ornaments seem to need paving, rather than say, a gravel path, but a sense of fitness will tell us what may be used and when and where.

Looking down the central lawn from the terrace there are flower borders on either side with, at the far end, delphiniums and phlox and *Nepeta faassenii* spreading on to and softening the lines of the paving. The colours of the delphiniums and the nepeta give, as blues do, a feeling of distance. Behind the flowers are rhododendrons, philadelphus, flowering cherries and other shrubs, all lovely in spring with their flowers and the charming soft greens of their young leaves, while later their darker foliage throws up the colours of the summer flowers. And they make a separate garden of the glade, distinct and quite different in character from the other gardens.

The glade, in its spring freshness, is like a piece of fairyland. In it there are Japanese maples and azaleas with colonies of lilies, white, yellow and orange, and some *Juniperus chinensis pfitzeriana*, the grey-green of which is such a charming foil for the lilies and other flowers near it. The red Japanese maples cannot be valued too highly because they are so lovely both in shape and colour and other colours seem to gain in value from being near them.

## *The value of trees and shrubs*

Anyone who has made one will have found out how much more interesting any garden is if it has some trees or shrubs of fair size in it. Trees and shrubs give light and shade and, what matters even more, they will separate the various parts which together make the complete garden. Some gardens are too small to divide, but imagine for a moment a more extensive garden of one space only. There is nothing to discover, no sense of mystery, it can all be seen at a glance!

Water, too, adds so much to the interest and charm of gardens. If there can be a formal pool which will in itself give the reason for some fountain figure, this will heighten interest tremendously. In the pool at Hillside there are water-lilies—the dwarf kinds, for the pool is small and only 2 feet deep. And goldfish add the finishing touch of life.

It was interesting to go to this garden on one visit and to see heaps of soil and clay everywhere so that one wondered if order would ever come out of the prevailing chaos, and on subsequent visits to see the heaps subsiding, the levels emerging, and later, when the

75

big rhododendrons were planted, to see formal gardens, walks and glade appear as if by magic. Rhododendrons are accommodating plants, with their close balls of roots large specimens can be moved safely and they give an air of furnished maturity at once, as if by waving a magic wand a garden suddenly appears. But that is only after a lot of hard preparatory work.

## INTRODUCING COLOUR

### Plate 39

At Langham Hall, near Colchester, the drive, passing the old church, goes between coniferous and other trees to the forecourt. From the forecourt the view, wide, and framed on both sides by forest trees, their branches sweeping the turf, extends down the length of the lawn, across the valley with the River Stour winding through it, and on to the low distant hills. It is a wonderful panorama of constantly changing lights and clouds and distance and is probably the reason why the house was so orientated.

But although the Hall and its immediate surroundings had the grandeur of mature trees and the spaciousness of extensive lawns it needed the colour and interest of gardens and flowers. To the east of the house there was level ground, again with a dense background of trees, not too near and yet giving the necessary shelter. This ground was overlooked by principal windows and it was here that gardens were made.

The rather narrow gravel path on to which the house had opened was replaced by a wider paved terrace and this, with flagstones laid against the dwarf stone walls, bordered a generous panel of lawn. Across the lawn there is the rose garden with all its richness of colour.

The rose garden, semicircular in plan, is enclosed at the back by a low stone wall, which, covered with aubrietas and thymes, is, early in the year, a background of crimson, pink and purple, against which the unfolding foliage of the roses tells so beautifully. And the wall, with a yew hedge on the higher level gives a welcome feeling of enclosure. But to go back to the forecourt with its view across the long stretch of mown turf to the almost limitless distance and then, turning the corner of the house to come into the sheltered, enclosed gardens is to see a noticeable contrast, the contrast of unbroken space with enclosed lawn and flower gardens.

### The use of ornaments

Central in the semicircle an Italian well-head with behind it a wrought iron gate, increases the slightly Italianate character of this garden. Perhaps the greatest difference between

English and Italian gardens is that in Italy stone seats, ornaments and statuary are as, if not more, important than flowers, while in Great Britain we have trees and lawns and a wealth of flowers, with few ornaments and those few carefully placed. Each is right in its own climate.

Through the iron gate there is a glade of flowering trees and shrubs in which, sheltered by conifers and forest trees, there are groups of azaleas, ceanothus with lilies, *Lilium testaceum*, a lovely shade of Nankeen yellow and the always distinctive *L. regale*, and, spreading on to the sward, *Juniperus chinensis pfitzeriana* and the lower-growing *J. sabina tamariscifolia*. One has to be careful how the colours of many flowers are grouped, but with lilies this is not so necessary and white, yellow, pink and even some scarlet varieties are quite lovely together, only there should be enough of them and they should be growing as if naturalised. Near the lilies are red Japanese acers, *A. palmatum atropurpureum* and *A. palmatum dissectum atropurpureum*, both rich crimson all the summer.

Between and separating the rose garden from the glade a herbaceous walk extends from the forecourt at one end to a tennis court at the other. Long and formal, the walk is a complete contrast to the curving lines of the glade bordering it on its southern length. In its borders there are hemerocallis, yellow heleniums, the tall flowers of delphiniums, the low growing santolina, rather for its cushions of grey foliage than for its flowers, rosemary, lavenders, *Artemisia abrotanum*, the fragrant southernwood, for its grey foliage and scent, and the taller *Artemisia lactiflora* with its plumes of creamy-white flowers. The broad stretches of colours on either side of the turf walk are at their best from June onwards.

## Backgrounds for flowers

Flowers look much more effective if they are seen against a dark background than if they are, as it were, standing in air. To make a comparison it is something like the difference between a picture on a wall or, as I have said earlier, a picture hanging in space. To the south of the flower walk there is the glade of hardy flowering trees and shrubs, so planned that the shrubs along its northern side are a background to the southern flower border. In this glade bush and standard flowering cherries, prunus, philadelphus, laburnums and lilacs grow high at the back (the white-flowered varieties, Edith Cavell and Mme Abel Chatenay against yellow laburnums) with, in front of them, weigela and deutzias. Covered with small white flowers in April, *Spiraea arguta* is charming with *Cytisus albus*, the white broom. The Spanish broom, *Spartium junceum*, produces its deep yellow flowers in July and flowers for a long time. Kniphofias, red-hot pokers, against *Cotinus coggygria foliis purpureis* and such berberis as *B. thunbergii* and *B. t. atropurpurea* together make glowing harmonies of colour. The red varieties of Japanese maples and other shrubs with purple foliage may be used with yellow and orange flowers to make the richest colour schemes.

And in yet another walk which, sheltered by trees and conifers, runs parallel with the big lawn on its eastern side, there are hardy rhododendrons and camellias, bridging the floral hiatus early in the year with their distinctive flowers. This walk leads to a pool—the subject of one of Constable's paintings, for Langham Hall stands in Constable country; in the Tate Gallery there are paintings of The Glebe Farm and Langham Church.

Turning to the west from the pool, steps from a sunken walk lead to the main lawn and to the house.

## A TERRACE OF THREE GARDENS
### Plates 40, 41

Stonely Woods is a long low house which opens on to a broad terrace. Symmetrical and rectangular, this terrace is enclosed by high stone walls, and, increasing the feeling of enclosure the side walls are returned for a short distance to sweep down in long curves to the breast high wall which forms its southern boundary. The long level line of this wall, in some mysterious way, enhances the beauty of the scenery beyond—hills which, standing high to the east, fall in gentle slopes to the richly wooded parkland to the south and west.

The terrace has been made into a formal garden, or rather into three gardens, each different from the others in the character of its planting, but each related to the others by the walks that extend from end to end of the terrace. From a door under the central gable of the house a wide flagged walk leads to a semicircular rotunda, which, with a built-in seat, projects into the park. From this seat the panorama of scenery and the wide arc of the ever-changing sky can be enjoyed together with the scents and colours of flowers that fill the terrace. Beds of iris and lavender, a symphony in grey, purple and mauve, a charming introduction to the flowers to either side of them, border the centre walk.

From a loggia at the western end of the house steps descend to the rose garden. Low-growing thymes and campanulas soften the hard lines of the paving and when the roses are in flower the garden is a scene of lovely colours and a mass of fragrant scents. Each bed, planted with one variety only in a colour scheme that has been carefully arranged; the garden is like a picture in a grey frame, the frame of lavender which fills the outer borders.

In the centre garden groups of shrubs with grey foliage, *Senecio laxifolius*, *Phlomis fruticosa*, rosemary and lavender, spread on to the paving. There are kniphofias or red-hot pokers, their reed-like foliage and stiff poker-like flowers a contrast to the plants with a less aggressive way of growing. There are hemerocallis in shades of orange, bronze, yellow and apricot, lovely against their grey neighbours, and hostas, as decorative for their large heart-shaped leaves as for their silvery-lilac flowers. And how beautiful the lilies standing erect behind them look, a harmony of white, pale yellow and grey.

78

In the eastern garden, again a complete change, both in habit and shape of plants and of colour, there are some standard roses and groups of *Rosa rubrifolia*, its misty pink right with almost any colour except strong yellows and orange. There are, too, *Rosa* Fantin Latour, growing 4 to 5 feet high and wider, its arching growths covered with large pink flowers; *R.* Charles de Mills, one of the finest of the gallicas, produces velvety, plum-coloured flowers, very full and 3 to 4 inches wide; *R.* Gloire de France, growing 3 feet high, with full blooms a lovely shade of lilac, deeper in the bud stage and later turning to palest mauve as the flowers open, and *R.* Cardinal de Richelieu, its flowers a rich dark shade of purple. There are other roses of earlier times, such as *R. violacea*, *R.* des Peintres and *R.* Black Damask. But I like best to stand at the end of the terrace and gaze at the sea of foliage and flowers, as though looking across the big marquee at the Chelsea Flower Show when it is a riot of colour before being finally tidied up and order emerges from apparent chaos—both fit subjects for a skilful painter.

## LINKING FEATURES
*Plate 42*

In extensive gardens the various parts that together make the complete garden should be so planned that there is harmonious contrast in their relation to each other. The nature of the site will determine to a considerable degree what these gardens should be, but almost invariably there should be one formal garden, if only as a contrast to the informal glades.

At The Vern near Hereford, a walled enclosure, formerly a kitchen garden, was made into a formal flower garden. The high wall on its northern side was swept down in a long curve to sitting height with the result that, although separate gardens, the flowers in the formal garden and the herbaceous walk mingle over the lower part of the wall to give the effect of one wide luxuriant border.

Paving from the terrace was extended into the new formal garden in which the central panel of lawn was set in paved paths. The flowers spreading on to the flagstones give a richer, more furnished appearance than would be the case if they were growing against turf.

An existing second kitchen garden was enlarged to provide additional space in which to grow fruit and vegetables. This facilitated the work in both kitchen garden and green-house.

## SPACIOUSNESS WITH STEPS
### Plates 43, 44

The Mill House, Fittleworth, Sussex, is built of stone and mellowed red brick. The wide paved terrace on the south front continues round the end of the building to connect with terraced gardens rising to the northern boundary wall. Had the site been level I felt that the main lawn, which extends from east to west for the length of the gardens with the river as its southern boundary, should have been carried round the return of the house on its eastern end. To do this was, however, impossible because of the difference in levels; the ground rises steeply, and to give as far as possible the feeling of space I designed the wide flight of shallow steps which ascends to the formal gardens. This flight of steps, together with the terrace walls, helps to continue the lines of the house into the garden and it creates an illusion of greater space than would otherwise be the case.

The old mill, although not now in use, is still standing in the grounds and it is from this and the mill stream that the Mill House derives its name.

## USING PAVING TO ADVANTAGE
### Plates 45, 46

Sheltered by trees, walls and hedges, Pilgrim's Cottage, Itchenor, is near the sea. The house, with white walls and thatched roof—and how happily the grey-brown of thatch tones with the off-white walls—stands near the southern boundary. The drive, passing the entrance front, goes on to a courtyard. But this is not only a courtyard, it is in itself an attractive part of the gardens. Enclosed on one side by an end wall of the house, on another by an old tiled barn, the courtyard is open to the lawns and gardens. Looking across its surface, panelled with York stone and cobbles, there are the mysterious dark shadows of the open barn, its posts draped with climbing roses and clematis; there are rhododendrons, high banks of colour when flowering through the summer and, heightening the charm of it all, the lovely unbroken vista down the length of the garden.

From the courtyard there is, skirting the western boundary, a straight walk, at the commencement of which, on a stone column, stands a small lead figure. This walk, so formal in its unbroken length, extends almost to the northern boundary. The planting in its flanking borders is first chiefly shrubs, amongst them lilacs, laburnums and brooms. The tall growing *Spartium junceum* is at the back with berberis in front of it to hide its rather bare stems, and the reddish-bronze of the berberis goes beautifully with the yellow

41. The rotunda and part of the terrace gardens at Stonely Woods

42. The Vern, near Hereford. Here the walled kitchen garden has been transformed into a formal
flower garden

43. The Mill House, Fittleworth, Sussex, from the river which forms its southern boundary

44. Lawn walk leading to wide paved terrace, at The Mill House, Fittleworth

45. Pilgrim's Cottage, Itchenor, with shrubs bordering the main lawn

46. The courtyard, panelled with York stone and cobbles, at Pilgrim's Cottage, Itchenor

47. Herbaceous
borders at
Hascombe Court,
Surrey

48. A villa on the
French Riviera,
showing the
spacious effect
given by paving

49. Hascombe Court—the upper terrace

flowers of *Spartium junceum*. There are several ornamental cherries, the white *Prunus* Tai-Haku chequers the turf with its shadows, and, farther on, laburnums which, too, go well with berberis. Farther still there is a more open space with flowers, the only herbaceous borders in the garden. A semicircular seat at the far end backed by a yew hedge is a fitting termination to the straight formality of the walk.

Near the barn on its northern side some old Scots pines stand like sentinels. Their trunks, in sunlight a warm red-brown crowned with flattish grey-green foliage clear cut against the sky, are lovely with the character that belongs to mature Scots pines. To cover the ground beneath them some *Pinus mugo* have been planted. This, however, is an experiment and it remains to be seen whether these pines will tolerate the shade of their taller relatives.

The centre glade at Pilgrim's Cottage is the loveliest part of the gardens. Near the house the glade is wide with standard cherries in it, their shadows like a patterned carpet with drifts of crocus, so welcome with their early colours, under them. Nearer the house, too, *Juniperus chinensis pfitzeriana* have become great flattish mounds of grey-green and there are Japanese maples crimson in colour and lovely in shape. By their growth the Japanese maples show their appreciation of their sheltered places and of the comparative mildness of the sea air.

## Colourful berberis

Although not perhaps so exclusively for the connoisseur, the berberis family embraces some very beautiful types and at Pilgrim's Cottage, *Berberis rubrostilla* and *B. stenophylla* have grown into banks of foliage, spreading and graceful in an altogether charming way. Covered in autumn with carmine-red translucent fruits and glowing autumn foliage *B. rubrostilla* is a mass of rich colour. There is, too, *B.* Pirate King and *B. verruculosa*, the rich glossy evergreen foliage of the latter so effective a contrast with the deciduous kind. There are *B. thunbergii*, bronze-green during the summer, a green that goes so well with all shades of yellow and orange, and its near relative *B. t. atropurpurea*, purple all the summer and even more brilliant in autumn. Nearer the house colonies of lilies, growing out of carpets of heathers, with the rich colours of Japanese acers, crimson during the summer and assuming even richer autumn shades, make this glade lovely all the summer and in the autumn a blaze of splendour.

The end of the glade curves, unexpectedly, into a rose garden. The site had been a kitchen garden but now, filled with roses and with a fine Italian well-head standing on paving in its centre, it is a garden of colour and fragrance, the finer by the contrast of its formal design with the informal curving borders of the glade.

## PAVING CREATING SPACIOUSNESS

*Sketch on page 101*

The lofty stone walls of a villa on the French Riviera rise high above the terrace and surrounding terrain. But because the ground fell steeply on the entrance front it was difficult to construct a forecourt. There was not the necessary level space. The drive was widened as far as the levels allowed, but it is a terrace rather than a forecourt. With their gnarled, twisted trunks and their many small grey leaves, olives are so lovely that two already in the forecourt had to be retained. To give the effect of making the space appear much larger the surface was paved in place of gravel or other material.

When possible, gardens gain very much if they can be visually related to the scenery beyond their boundaries and here the olives in the paving beautifully link the formality of the terrace with the grey feathery foliage of the olives beneath. Rising sentinel-like against the walls, the tall cypresses, so typical of Provence, by the contrast of their dark vertical lines, add a dramatic note to the scene.

## VARIETY IN DESIGN AND COLOUR

*Plates 5, 13, 47, 49*

Built partly in the local Bargate stone and the remainder in red brick and half timber, Hascombe Court stands on a level plateau. From this plateau the ground formerly fell steeply to a rock garden on the southern slope. This gave the uneasy impression that the house was perched on the edge of a precipice and might slide over. Terraces and steps can, when necessary, add so much to the interest of gardens and a second terrace was built on the steep slope from the upper terrace on the south front. This terrace, paved, with panels of brick inset in the flagstones, extends beyond the house both to the east and west and appears to set the house firmly on its base. Semicircular seats built into the walls at either end, and a semicircular pool recessed into the wall which supports the higher level, with water falling into the basin from a carved lion's head, add considerably to the interest of the terrace. This, the middle terrace, enclosed on three sides by stone walls and to the south by a stone balustrade, with its flower-filled borders, with clipped yews at regular intervals to emphasise the design, is really a formal flower garden. Steps from it go down to a third terrace, comparatively narrow and planted as a lavender walk. This walk, too, is paved and from it yet more steps lead to the rock garden. The effect of these terraces is heightened by their contrasting design and orderly sequence, the middle one being the widest and most elaborate.

The herbaceous borders at Hascombe Court are a noticeable feature. As they were, these borders showed no sense of colour harmony, strong pinks quarrelled with oranges and yellows, there was no gradation of colour and the result was a discordant muddle. The borders were emptied and replanted to a carefully prepared colour scheme. There was no formal flower garden and there was little contrast of design in the various walks and gardens as they were.

Just as in a symphony a slow movement can be introduced to emphasise the qualities of other movements, so, in gardens, will a walk or garden of soft colours, blue, mauve, lavender for instance, intensify the richer colours of adjacent gardens. For this reason and also because blue flowers can be so lovely in themselves, the borders on each side of a walk connecting the upper terrace with a formal paved garden were planted with delphiniums, purple salvias and the blue-mauve *Nepeta faassenii*. As a contrast to the grouped plants in the formal paved garden, these borders were planted formally in straight rows.

## A succession of colour

The paved garden which is, so to speak, the drawing room of the gardens, has a lily pool with moulded stone coping and in its centre a fine fountain group in lead. Its borders are filled with tulips in the spring, followed in their season by blue and pink bedding petunias, the ruby-red *Penstemon* Southgate Gem, and ivy-leaved geraniums, growing luxuriantly over the flagstones. Taller behind them permanent backgrounds of delphiniums, *Romneya coulteri*, ceanothus, lavender, rosemary and other plants give a succession of harmonious colour. The formal design of this garden is accentuated by the close growing *Juniperus communis hibernica* planted symmetrically in the angles of the paving.

Before the gardens were altered the long glade was uncultivated ground. There were Scots and Austrian pines in scattered groups, lupins and gorse grew everywhere, but there were a few well grown firs and silver birches. The undergrowth was cleared, and lawns extending in a long sweeping curve to a terrace, constructed on the southern boundary, were sown. The pines, birches and cedars left growing in the turf add to the charm of the glade.

On the eastern boundary of the new glade there was already a belt of Scots and Austrian pines which protected and made an excellent background for the shrubs and plants in the borders. Magnolias were planted, their distinctive flowers and handsome leaves showing in high relief against the dark backgrounds. Japanese maples in their sheltered quarters have grown into mounds of colour; *Juniperus chinensis pfitzeriana* had space in which to attain its full size. There were azaleas, with hardy lilies amongst them; there were spiraeas and *Cytisus albus*, deutzia and weigela, all in groups large enough for each to reveal its distinctive character. The long glade was a complete contrast to the formal gardens, to the straight lines of the herbaceous walks and to the equally formal though less elaborate terrace which was built at its southern end.

## Creating a vista

On its western front the house opens on to a paved terrace, sheltered by two projecting wings of the house. From it, across the lawn one sees the colours of the herbaceous borders between which a mown turf walk extends to the western boundary. Near the boundary there was formerly a small circular sunken pool enclosed by tall yew hedges which completely shut off the extensive views on to the scenery beyond. The hedges were removed, the rather dank looking pool demolished and the lovely wooded distance came into view. The borders on either side of this walk were planted in a colour scheme of soft pink, blue, mauve, purple and pale yellow, with grey-foliaged plants, and a few small groups of white flowers. At its western end *Senecio laxifolius* grows over the low walls and on to circular steps which descend to a turf walk, which leads between borders of azaleas to the rhododendron wood.

The wood was already in existence. It was on a sloping hillside facing south and it was fairly dense. A number of trees were felled, leaving enough oaks and birches with an occasional fir standing well apart so that they cast light intermittent shade, conditions so suitable for rhododendrons. Bordering the walks which were cleared through the wood, many of the good hardy hybrids were planted, while on the lower slopes *R. barbatum*, *R. arboreum*, *R. fortunei*, *R. falconeri*, *R. thompsonii*, *R. grande*, as well as the early flowering *R. praecox* and others of the finer hybrids and species, grow well. The ground under and amongst the rhododendrons is carpeted with heaths. An unusual feature here is a stone stairway which ascends from the rhododendron wood to a walk planted on each side with camellias. Tall bamboos on both sides arch over and chequer the flagstones of the stairway with patterns of light and shade.

There is usually an affinity between the colours of the different species and varieties of any particular plant genus, but the colours of some of the Ghent and Mollis azaleas clash with the colours of many rhododendrons. At Hascombe Court numbers of azaleas are grown under the light shade of trees leading to the rhododendron walks, but the two are not seen together.

## Visual relation of garden to scenery

Gardens can sometimes be visually related to the near scenery with the happiest results and to achieve this, distant contours might be continued unbroken into the gardens. Trees growing naturally in the district, if repeated in the garden, would establish a continuity, a relation between the gardens and the country beyond. Such trees could, if suitable, be used to form background or boundary planting. At Hascombe Court groups of *Tsuga canadensis* and pines were planted in the glade borders to frame vistas and, as it were, echo the firs on the distant hills.

From the rhododendron wood turf walks lead to the rock garden, the sunlit open space of which gains so much in value by contrast with its shaded approaching ways. As it was, the rock garden was not bold enough in its conception and the stones used in its construction were too small; its paths were too narrow and it had little relation to the gardens as a whole, or to the landscape. The obvious treatment here seemed to be a rock garden, and in the new one, built of proportionately large stones, the contours of the valley below were carried back to it, with an increasing curve until the water-worn stone with which it was built rose almost vertically to support the outer wall of the south terrace. By carrying the contours of the valley into this garden a subtle and pleasing continuity and relation between it and the landscape was established.

Standing on the flight of steps that descends from the second terrace one looks down the length of Brenda's Walk which, skirting the valley, goes in a long curve to a rotunda built on the southern boundary. In its eastern border laburnums mingle with silver birches and *Parrotia persica* gives, even early in the year, a foretaste of the richness of its late summer and autumn dress. There are sweet briars, Lord and Lady Penzance, with fawn and copper flowers; groups of *Berberis stenophylla* grow taller at the back and *B. verruculosa* contrasts beautifully with the deciduous *B. rubrostilla* and *B. thunbergii* near it. Other shrubs here are the early flowering *Mahonia bealei* and several groups of hypericums all adding to the general harmony of orange, bronze, yellow and green. These colours are made even richer by the yellow and orange flowers of hardy lilies.

Before the gardens were remade and extended, the straight drive passed through serried ranks of tightly packed rhododendrons, to turn at right angles into the forecourt. Although there was ample space on both sides, the approach appeared narrow and characterless. The rhododendrons were removed. Wide borders of mown turf were laid on either side of the gravelled drive and columnar conifers were planted in groups at the back of the mown turf. Douglas firs, *Chamaecyparis lawsoniana allumii* and *C.* Triomphe de Boskoop and the distinctive *Juniperus chinensis* and *J. chinensis aurea* now frame a spacious avenue with, at its far end, wrought iron gates through which one sees the trees and flowers of the gardens. The drive is a dignified composition of vertical and horizontal lines.

From the drive there is a long, straight herbaceous walk, terminated at its eastern end by an open-fronted summer-house. Looking from it there is a continuous vista from the eastern to the western boundaries of the gardens. But as a change from the western herbaceous walk, which was planted in a scheme of pink, mauve, grey and other soft shades, these borders have blue and purple delphiniums, orange heliopsis, yellow and bronze heleniums, purple salvias, crimson monarda, scarlet *Lychnis chalcedonica* and many other herbaceous plants, together making a brilliant display of colour during summer and autumn.


## INTEREST WITHIN THE GARDEN BOUNDARIES
### Plates 14, 50

In some gardens it is possible to relate the principal vistas to the scenery beyond, and there are others in which interest has to be created within the garden boundaries. Enclosed by belts of Scots pines, silver birches and tall rhododendrons dense enough to give excellent backgrounds for the flowers and shrubs, the gardens at Westwoods, Surrey, are entirely private.

Some gardens may be kept private by separating them from the drive and forecourt by hedges or other suitable planting. Others can be made to look finer and more extensive if the drive and forecourt are treated as an integral part of the gardens. At Westwoods a new drive was made close to banks of tall rhododendrons on one side, while from the other one looked into a glade which extends for the length of the site on its western boundary. The drive makes an approach to the forecourt, the beauty of which would have been very much lessened had it been a separate entity. And, looking down the glade, the view disappearing between pines and rhododendrons, one gets a foretaste of the gardens.

The forecourt at Westwoods was paved and enclosed by low stone retaining walls built when the gardens were remade and extended. With rhododendrons growing over the walls it is a spacious setting for the house.

Before the gardens were remodelled there was, on the eastern side of the house, a lawn enclosed by rhododendrons. It was a debatable point whether to remove or to leave a fine copper beech, which blocked a principal view from the house but, after due consideration and recognising the fact that it could be felled at any time, the beech was left. On the south front a flight of steps from the upper terrace led down to a second terrace, from which yet another circular flight of steps descended to the orchard, kitchen garden and a herbaceous border. Below the kitchen garden was a pool, the overflow from which disappeared into wild undergrowth near the southern boundary. Westwoods did not lend itself to the making of formal gardens. Its potential beauty was in the slopes and undulations of the ground, in open spaces, in long vistas and walks, and in its beautiful setting of Scots pines, birches and rhododendrons.

The existing kitchen garden which, previous to the alterations was seen from windows and terraces, obviously could not be left where it was. With the glasshouses and frames the kitchen garden was moved to ground near the northern boundary of the estate, and the space thus cleared made into a lawn. This lawn, sweeping into the outer glades with masses of colour on all sides is really the heart or centre of the gardens.

## A rhododendron walk

Thickets of *Rhododendron ponticum*, previously growing on the eastern side of the house, were removed and a lawn sown to curve round into a walk which, long and straight, extends through Scots pines to the pool at its lower end. Amongst and in front of the pines this walk, some 30 feet wide, was planted on both sides with newer varieties of rhododendrons, the foliage of which, growing on to the turf, is naturally beautiful even when they are not in flower. Lengthening the flowering season there are numbers of pink, crimson and purple ericas, a richly coloured ground covering. With its green banks of rhododendrons, lawn carpet and reflecting water shining at the lower end of its gradual slope this walk is a delightful contrast to the informal gardens.

To the east, at the lower end of the walk, a piece of ground was made into an azalea garden. The ground was cleared, some birches, their silvery trunks and pendant lacy foliage so right with the azaleas, were left and backgrounds of Scots pines and other conifers were planted. A wide turf walk was made through it and the borders planted with yet more azaleas. It is a sea of colour and fragrant with scent while the azaleas are flowering and later there is the richness of their autumn foliage.

Looking from the upper terrace across the centre lawn, one sees on all sides banks of rhododendrons, rose species, the rich purple of *Cotinus coggygria foliis purpureis*, philadelphus, and other flowering shrubs growing around it. The falling contours of the ground are lovely. Water shining in the distance gives reflections of trees and, when they are in flower, a wealth of colour from the rhododendrons mirrored in it. The turf walk alongside the lake disappears between Scots pines and birches to appear again on the far side.

From here the stream, which formerly disappeared into wild undergrowth, was widened to make a lower pool, shallow but fairly extensive, into which the overflow from the upper pool falls over boulders of water-worn stone, a miniature waterfall. From the spreading branches of *Juniperus chinensis pfitzeriana*, against a background of yet more Scots pines and silver birches, there are dark lines of shadow under which the stone seems to belong naturally to the site. It is a picture of lighted water losing itself in mysterious shadows. Several islands, with moisture-loving plants and birches and rhododendrons growing on them, break its level surface. Here and there a water-worn stone, like an outcrop of submerged rock, rises from the water. The lawns of the east and west glades, both of which continue to the lower pool, are connected by mown turf around its farther end, giving a continuous way round the water. Flanking the turf walks the borders, planted with dwarf abies and spruce, low-growing junipers, mollis azaleas, deutzias, weigela and other flowering shrubs, form a natural setting for the lower sheet of water.

## Tamed woodland

The western glade, in contrast to the broad walk on the eastern side of the gardens with its straight boundaries, is irregular in outline. On each side banks of rhododendrons spread luxuriantly on to the turf. There are Scots pines, their branches pendulous with the weight of grey-green foliage and lovely in the way of mature trees. Here and there a pine breaks away from its companions to stand by itself in the turf and throws its chequered pattern on to the sward beneath. There are silver birches and an occasional cherry. It is like looking into a clearing in a wood, only a wood that, with its carpet of mown turf, has had its natural wildness tamed. Nowhere is there a straight line, for the rhododendrons grow as they like and the turf is mown to suit them. But fine as they are, the pines created their own difficulties, for soil that is made of accumulations of many years of pine needles is not good for lawns and the topsoil had to be removed and replaced with fertile material. Wide openings were cut through from the glade to the centre lawn, giving extensive vistas across the lawn and up and down the glade. At its northern end the glade widens into a lawn enclosed by pines, silver birches and rhododendrons, a scene of contrasting light and shade and with the light-reflecting surface of a pool. From this lawn stone steps, built between the trees, ascend to the terrace.

There was at Westwoods a stream, the water falling in a series of rockbound pools into the larger pools near the southern boundary. With stepping stones laid in the turf, the stream walk between banks of rhododendrons is shady, a contrast to the open spreading lawns.

The greater number of gardens need some formal treatment if only to heighten, by its contrast, the beauty of their informal walks and glades, but at Westwoods the only formal feature introduced was a rose garden to the south-east of the house. It is bounded for its length on one side by the curving stone wall built to sitting height, which gives, as it were, a continuation on a lower level of the architectural lines of the house. This wall, with the flagging from which it rises, forms a resting-place from which to overlook the still lower central lawn with its surrounding masses of plants and colour. Although formal, the rose garden was designed as a long continuous curve so that some fine rhododendrons bordering it on its northern side could be retained.

In making the gardens at Westwoods my aim was to heighten as much as possible the natural beauties of the site. With water flowing through the grounds from the north-west

50. A paved path and steps leading down to the lower lawns at Westwoods, Surrey

51. Pools, canal and fountains at Westfields, Bedfordshire

52. The informal water garden at Westfields

53. Dartington Hall, Devon. The great stairway which connects the upper glade and the lower lawn

54. The azalea dell at Dartington Hall

55. The magnificent view from the highest terrace at Dartington Hall

56. Upper part of the river garden at Monteviot, near Jedburgh

57. View of river from arched wall-shelter at Monteviot

58. A garden glade at Chestham Park, Sussex

59. *Chamaecyparis lawsoniana allumii* line the walk from the rose garden to the tennis courts at Chestham Park

to the southern boundary, and with the spacious central lawn and continuous outer glades, varying both in their form and in the character of their planting, it was possible to give these gardens the charm of varied and lovely scenery.

## DIFFERENT STYLES WITH WATER
*Plates 8, 15, 16, 51, 52*

Approached by a long drive, Westfields stands in the village of Oakley near Bedford, in a pleasantly secluded position more or less in the centre of its own woodlands and park-like meadows. Before the gardens were altered there were lawns on which several limes and other trees gave a feeling of age. There was, too, a tennis court, a formal lawn enclosed within low brick walls. As it was the garden was neither extensive nor interesting enough to be in keeping with the size and character of the house. It had no highlights, no un-expected changes of scene, it was monotonous. But the opportunities were there. I asked for more land beyond the present northern boundary as this would enable me to make finer contrasts in the relation of the various gardens.

Additional lawns and glades were turfed and planted, a rose garden was made at the end of the lawn on to which the house opens and the tennis court was changed into an informal water garden. It may seem unusual to have an informal water garden in an entirely rectangular space but the design I prepared for a natural stream in which the water, crossing the garden diagonally, fell from one to another of a series of pools was decided upon. The natural stream garden was made to end in a large pool extending into the main lawn and was thus brought into view from the principal windows.

As one approaches the house, lawns and vistas spread in various directions. To the right there is the lowest rock-bound pool, rising to the upper pools, the water circulating by means of an electric pump. With backgrounds of shrubs, deutzias, weigelas, *Cytisus albus* and *C. praecox*, with cypresses to give density, and cotoneasters because they will grow under trees where many other shrubs will not, the water garden is a separate garden. There were, too, some old standard thorns which helped to screen it from the adjoining gardens and the lawn sweeping into the glades at either end adds by its continuity to the charm of the gardens as a whole. Its banks confined by Westmorland stone, with its water-worn channels, the stream is like a fragment of mountain scenery, only with the colours of flowers reflected in it.

In this water garden there are Japanese iris, as well as a number of their not quite so dis-tinguished relatives. But the *germanica* branch of the iris family can claim a very con-siderable number of fine varieties. There are hostas growing well in the moist soil and primulas, and in the higher borders farther away from the stream Japanese maples spreading over boulders which are covered with aubrietias and thymes in their varying shades of mauve, pink, crimson and purple. Cushions of *Juniperus sabina tamariscifolia* fill the spaces between the blocks of Westmorland stone. There are, too, groups of astilbes, the deep red *A.* Fanal and A. W. Reeves, and there are pink ones and White Queen. There are primulas growing close to the water, amongst them *P.* Red Hugh, *P. pulverulenta* Bartley strain, in a range of soft pinks, and the later *P. florindae*, a most attractive soft shade of yellow flowering in July and August. Here and there *Juniperus chinensis pfitzeriana* throws long branches over the water. The pools set in verdure-covered boulders combine to make a natural and attractive water garden.

## Water used formally

That part of the estate which, previous to the alterations, had been the forecourt is enclosed on both sides by brick walls. No longer necessary as a forecourt this is now a part of the gardens. The owner wished for a water garden here and with its straight boundaries of brick walls it should be formal—there was already the informal stream garden in the old tennis court. Two pools were constructed. The smaller of the two and nearer the house is square and is connected with the larger pool by a long canal or rill. Standing on the terrace the long stretch of water carries the eye into the far distance of park-like meadows studded with forest trees. A small lead figure in the nearer pool and a stone basin and figure standing high in the larger pool add the interest of falling water. To increase the formality of the design and to give colour, straight borders extend for the length of the garden on both sides. These borders are planted chiefly with old-fashioned and species roses—rhododendrons would have given more substance and been preferable but the soil is alkaline and rhododendrons could not be grown. There are, too, cotoneasters and elaeagnus for their evergreen foliage in winter, with groups of peonies, delphiniums and phlox to flower during summer. Mirrored in the water, the effect of colour is intensified and there are the floating leaves and lovely flowers of the water-lilies.

At Westfields it can be seen how gardens different in character and appearance can be related in one garden in an entirely pleasing way. From the principal garden door there is a view between groups of spreading *Juniperus chinensis pfitzeriana* to wrought iron gates through which, framed by plantations of forest trees, the vista is lost in distance.

Central on the length of the lawn and partly hidden under the shade of spreading branches of mature forest trees there is the red brick house. Borders are filled with flowering shrubs and herbaceous flowers give bold groups of colour. The long lawn leads to a rose garden, paved, and with a lily pool and fountain as its central feature.

From the centre of this lawn wide steps lead up to a glade of flowering trees and shrubs which extends from the eastern boundary to sweep unbroken into the water garden at its western end, a long vista changing in the character of its planting in all its length. In the borders *Ceanothus* Gloire de Versailles mingling with *Romneya coulteri* are lovely together. There is *Cytisus praecox* with *C. battandieri* growing taller behind it. Although, so to speak first cousins, *C. praecox* and *C. battandieri* are very different both in their habit of growth and in their flowers. And, like a sharp note of exclamation, the vertical columnar *Chamaecyparis lawsoniana allumii* rises from a low cushion of *Genista hispanica*. Farther on between the spreading growths of *Juniperus chinensis pfitzeriana* there is the informal water garden and the western glade.

From this glade the lawn sweeps into a straight walk which again extends for the length of the gardens from east to west. *Chamaecyparis lawsoniana allumii* at regular intervals, growing taller from the lower shrubs, add to the formality of this walk, in itself a fitting termination to the gardens on their northern boundary.

In the glades where, but for the alkalinity of the soil rhododendrons and azaleas would have been so suitable, there are banks of *Cotinus coggygria foliis purpureis*, lovely in itself and forming a wonderful background for other colours. In front of it are *Hypericum patulum* and *H. Hidcote*. The yellows of the shrubby hypericums are deep and yet without any trace of harshness. And they flower in summer. There are too, a number of philadelphus in its many varieties, single and double, which continue to flower through July and into August. There are shrub roses and, in a curve at the east end of the north walk, laburnums hang their long yellow racemes over the horizontal flower-laden branches of *Viburnum tomentosum mariesii*, one of the finest of the viburnums.

## FINE VISTAS

*Plates 53, 54, 55*

Dartington Hall stands in some of Devon's finest scenery. The drive from the public road to the hall is bordered by richly timbered pastures, rising to the south and on the north sloping down to the River Dart which, seen between ancient oaks and beeches, gives the final beauty to the scene.

The hall, firmly seated on the highest terrace, overlooks the principal gardens and the old tilting yard. This, low and enclosed by steep banks rising like giant steps, was an integral part of the domain and could not be altered. Dartington Hall was not for the more conventional type of garden. It demanded landscape on a grand scale, spreading lawns so that the magnificent trees—beeches, oaks and chestnuts—could be seen in all their glory, and the gardens needed long vistas into the surrounding park-like country. To make a principal vista an overgrown slope on the southern boundary was cleared except for the trees, which fortunately standing well back, helped to enclose a new glade which was made here. Walking down the glade from the highest point one sees, framed by trees and shrubs on either side, one of the finest views in the gardens.

At its lower end there is a great stairway. This, constructed when the gardens were altered, connects the new glade with the lower lawn and with the lovely parkland which has recently been brought into the orbit of the gardens.

Yet another long vista has recently been opened. From the northern end of the tilting yard the vista now extends down wide steps into and down the length of the tilting yard, down another flight of steps at the southern end into parkland, studded with ancient oaks and beeches. A stream runs through the centre of the meadow and it has not yet been decided whether the water should be dammed at the lowest level to make a small lake. With an adequate supply, water would undoubtedly add very much both to the beauty and interest of Dartington Hall.

As well as creating new ones, care has been taken to keep any existing vistas at Darting-ton Hall. Carpets of narcissi spread on each side of a wide mown turf walk from the old drive to the azalea dell, with a glimpse of the great hall between the giant beeches.

## THE FORMALITY OF LEVELS
### *Plates 9, 56, 57*

In some gardens interest has to be created within the garden boundaries, in others, views, sometimes extensive, sometimes more limited, have to be taken into account.

At Monteviot, near Jedburgh in Scotland, the house stands on a plateau overlooking the River Teviot flowing in the valley beneath. The gardens are of necessity terraced and a walk, long, straight and formal on the highest terrace has the effect of unifying the varying architectural styles of the house. The highest terrace is enclosed by yew hedges for approx-imately one-third of its length at each end. The centre length, without hedges, leaves the view open to the lovely river scenery. This centre length was, before the alterations, a slope, too steep to walk down and it gave an uncomfortable feeling that the upper terrace was not adequately supported. The reason for the slope was apparent—to leave the views from the house on to the river unbroken. But the house needed the formality of levels and this slope has now been changed into three terraces, the centre one noticeably the widest. The result of this treatment is that while the level terraces give the feeling of stability the views from the windows are uninterrupted.

It is at the western end of the upper terrace that flower gardens are made. From the long walk steps lead down to yet another walk still high above the lower gardens. There is a rose garden below a massive high wall. This garden is enclosed at each end by stone walls and yew hedges. It is paved and, open to the south, it is a sheltered sun trap. Beyond the rose garden is the river garden, so named because it leads directly to the river.

From an alcove recessed into the high wall that forms the northern boundary of the river garden, an avenue of cherries, *Prunus sargentii*, has been planted. This variety was chosen because it is upright in its habit and the colours of the generously wide borders can be seen between the trunks; *P. sargentii* is also one of the finest cherries for autumn colour. The avenue of prunus and the formal lines of the borders lead one's eye to a landing stage, from which wide stone steps descend to the river. Still to be built, the landing stage, paved and with heraldic beasts on piers at each end of its curving stone walls, will form the termination to, and make the walk from the alcove to the river, one garden. But it is not altogether a garden, for near the river the treatment merges into the landscape of the park and into a walk which borders the river to the west—a gradual transition from gardens to park.

At Monteviot there is the varying scenery of woodlands and wide spaces of turf, a green setting in which it would be difficult to have too much colour. And in the river garden, on each side there are parallel borders, the colours of which show so effectively between the trunks of the prunus. In the near borders on each side low flowering shrubs and groups of floribunda roses flower for a long time, while in the outer borders flowering trees and shrubs—lilacs, laburnums, deutzias, shrub roses, *Spartium junceum* and *Cytisus battandieri* for their summer flowers—build up to frame the wide centre turf walk in masses of rich colour. Walks of turf 20 feet wide between double borders on each side add to the interest of the garden.

## GLADES AND BROAD WALKS
### Plates 58, 59, 60

The drive at Chestham Park in Sussex, when I first saw it, ran through an avenue of limes directly into the forecourt. The gardens and forecourt were, so to speak, one. The site was level. There were fine old trees, including some oaks, but as they were, the gardens showed little design and there was not enough colour. Colour can be produced quickly but trees take a long time to grow.

In its main idea the plan for the new gardens consists of broad walks and formal gardens contrasting with extensive glades of flowering trees and shrubs. A principal walk, long and wide in proportion, extending from a sun room to the eastern boundary, is terminated by a semicircular stone seat, the level back of which enhances the scenic value of the distant park trees. Columnar chamaecyparis, planted on either side of the seat when the gardens were altered, frame, like a distant picture, the vista into the park. On each side there is a draped life-sized stone figure on a stone base and these, light against the dark chamaecyparis, could belong to some Italian garden. Only the picture gains so much from its foreground of green turf. In Italy gravel would probably replace the turf—not nearly so effectively.

## Influence of Italian design

The slightly Italianate feeling given by the seat and stone figures is repeated in a walk from the tennis courts to the rose garden. This walk, enclosed on both sides by yew hedges, has at intervals on each side *Chamaecyparis lawsoniana allumii*. To obtain as nearly as possible the effect of Italian cypress, which would have been so effective but which do not grow well in England, the chamaecyparis have been trimmed into the narrow shape characteristic of their Italian relatives. The walk, a green interlude between the herbaceous borders and the rose garden, heightens by its contrast the colour values of both. Enclosed by yew hedges, the rose garden is large and has in it a good selection of the best tea and hybrid tea roses, each variety in its separate bed. Spreading into it on its eastern side a cedar, too fine to be removed, has been left, its branches sweeping the turf. The cedar is still growing and spreading, an unusual feature in a rose garden.

On its south, formerly the entrance front, the house opens, first on to a wide flagged terrace and thence on to extensive lawns. Tall banks of rhododendrons stand far back and there are groups of hypericum and other shrubs, with delphiniums and dahlias to flower after the rhododendrons. From here the lawn sweeps behind the rose garden into another, wider glade in which, under a group of beeches, standing more or less in the centre, and again showing Italian influence on English design, a stone temple has recently been erected. The temple, with its classical figure forming a focal point from several vistas, is a charming note in its informal setting. It is not, however, to sit in but is an example of how such an ornament can, by the contrast of its formal lines with the surrounding trees and shrubs, heighten the beauty of a garden.

## Interest of water

Except for a lily pool in an enclosed garden near the house, the grounds at Chestham Park lacked the interest of water and, crossing the long walk, a water garden, made in what was formerly a rather wild part of the grounds, comes into view. The water falls from the nearest pool through a series of smaller pools varying in size and shape and bounded by water-worn Westmorland stone, grey, mossy and lovely, to disappear at the farther end of the garden. On its eastern side mown turf follows the irregular lines of boulders which lie like natural outcrops on some moorland valley. There are water-lilies in the pools with here and there the sword-like growths of rushes making so effective a contrast with the level water and with the leaves of the water lilies lying on its surface. The shapes of *Iris kaempferi* and *I. germanica* on the stream side echo those of the upright rushes growing in the water, and there are colonies of primulas and *Juniperus chinensis pfitzeriana*, throwing dark shadows, with flattish cushions of *J. sabina tamariscifolia* between the stone boulders. Thus the informal water garden is an unexpected change from the broad walks and glades of the gardens.

Goldfish, swimming with that easy grace that belongs to fish, give the final interest of life, without which no water seems complete. One wonders if the goldfish could, like salmon, leap up the miniature falls or do they stay in the particular pool in which they find themselves? I do not know. But they increase in numbers and the upper pools seem to be as thickly populated as the lower ones.

On the western side of the watercourse the turf is wider, a generous stretch of lawn which, curving to the right at the farther end of the garden, leads into yet another glade and from there to the long walk and to the house. The borders surrounding this glade are planted with shrub roses, philadelphus, weigelas, cherries, deutzias and other flowering trees and shrubs.

A new forecourt was made to one side of the house. Hedges of *Chamaecyparis lawsoniana allumii* were planted and these, with a wrought iron gate to give access from the drive, made the gardens private. Even a single tree can give character to its surroundings and at Chestham Park an old Scots pine, its trunk bare of branches and the rich shade of reddish-brown that Scots pines with age become, crowned with dark green branches and standing in an island of turf, dominates the forecourt. Another interesting feature is a small building, like some ancient monument but probably a dairy, built of half-timbered brick and roofed with tiles, the remains of some farmhouse of earlier times. Spacious, surrounded with buildings and walls behind borders of turf, the new forecourt has unusual character.

In making gardens we leave the realms of nature to enter the realms of art and even in glades, wild gardens and informal water gardens, there should be a niceness of balance, both of form and colour, that lifts the garden into the quality of those more rarified realms.

When gardens first came into being they were little more than beds and borders in turf. Through the years they have become more elaborate and one of the finest attributes of gardens of the present day lies in the skilful interweaving of formal and informal design in the same garden. This is particularly the case at Chestham Park.

## MERGING COLOUR SCHEMES

*Plate 61*

Architecturally, Milton, near Peterborough, is one of the finest houses in the country. The main north front dates from the late Elizabethan period, but there are signs of an earlier house having existed. The walls of the entrance front rise from the spacious forecourt with nothing to lessen the glory of the architecture. The park, which was laid out by Humphry Repton in 1791, is extensive and well wooded. Ancient oaks, elms, beeches and other trees, amongst them some London planes and cedars, diversify the park landscape.

The south elevation commands views, framed on either side by forest trees, which seem to extend almost to the horizon. There are no flower gardens in sight but near the house parterres of red floribunda roses give splashes of colour, vivid against the surrounding trees and turf.

*Colour borders*

From the left of the terrace a gravelled walk leads through dark masses of yews to the orangery, a Palladian building commanding views across the lake and into the park beyond. There were no flower gardens but on the way to the orangery handsome wrought iron gates led into what was formerly the larger of the walled gardens. A yew hedge has been planted to divide a part of this garden. Enclosed on three sides by high brick walls and on the fourth by the yew hedge, now grown thick and tall, this ground has been made into a formal flower garden. In it steps at each end lead down to a long sunken turf walk. There are flower borders on both sides of the walk, carefully arranged in a series of colour schemes, for one group of colour merges into another so that the borders are a succession of harmonious colours from end to end. Enclosed by walks following the lines of the old red brick walls and the hedge that together enclosed the whole, this centre has been changed into a formal sunken flower garden.

Between this garden and the outer enclosing walls there are separate borders of flowers; a paeony border, a border of phlox, an iris border, borders of roses—and an aster border. These borders are arranged in a definite colour scheme or rather several colour schemes, each merging into the next in such a way as to make a succession of pleasing colour groups. There are mounds of *Senecio laxifolius*, lavender, rosemary and *Phlomis fruticosa* and the low-growing *P. samia*. Grey foliage softens and makes otherwise discordant colours harmonious, and varieties of cistus and other shrubs planted on the higher borders grow over the low walls to mingle with the flowers in the sunken borders, thus making these borders appear even wider than they are.

60. Chestham Park—long formal walk from the house to the eastern boundary

61. A formal walled flower garden at Milton, Peterborough

62. The lower gardens at Falkland Palace, Fife

63. Cypresses lining
the long walk at
Lower Sandhill,
Sussex

64. The terrace on
the south front of
the house at Lower
Sandhill

65. Sketch for cloisters, formal pool and shelter at Llannerch Park

66. Llannerch Park, showing the paved terrace, long steps and canal after completion

It is a surprise to come on to this garden, sheltered by its high brick walls, full of colour and fragrance, gaining so much by its contrast with the surrounding greens of the trees and turf of the park.

## EMPHASISING THE HISTORICAL PAST
*Plate 62*

Falkland Palace, the hunting palace of the romantic Stuart dynasty, was perhaps more of a royal home than a place of state. Here beneath the Lomonds' twin 'paps of Fife', the Stuart kings and queens came to relax. Here they spent their leisure in archery and tennis. They rode out hawking with their hooded falcons in the park. They hunted stags through the glades and wild boar among the great oaks of the Forest of Falkland. At night they banqueted and played chess, to the soft music of fiddles and lutes. They were lovers of literature, and poets their welcome guests. Verses still recall those happy days of 'dancin and deray' long ago at 'Falkland on the Grene'.

The entrance to the courtyard is through an arch between the towers of the gatehouse. Rectangular in shape, this courtyard, which is overlooked by the windows of the long gallery and of the private apartments, is enclosed by the north range and on the east by the ruins of the old banqueting hall, the walls of which are still standing, but roofless and with the apertures of its windows open to the sky.

From the palace windows views extend beyond the courtyard over wooded terraces to the eastern boundary. The descending terraces were a succession of unvarying greens and to provide colour a formal paved flower garden has been made in the rectangular space within the foundations of the old north range, the walls of which are still plainly visible about 2 feet above ground level. Other than this garden there were no flower gardens at the Palace of Falkland.

The new gardens were designed to retain and to throw into higher relief the palace as it is at present and also, because of their architectural and historic interest, to preserve and bring into the scheme those traces that remain of the earlier, more extensive, palace. To accentuate what remains of the walls, part of the original buildings, columnar growing chamaecyparis have been planted at regular intervals on the higher levels. The effect of these conifers rising above the walls should, when they have attained their full height, form an effective composition of horizontal and vertical lines as well as emphasising the plan of former buildings.

To connect the new gardens with the courtyard, steps were constructed to lead down from the formal flower garden to a flagged terrace, which was made along the top of the

G

lower garden wall. This terrace, enclosed on the north by a low stone wall, leads at its farther end to stone steps, which, already in existence, descend to the recently made lower gardens. These, now the principal pleasure grounds, were designed to have a central glade extending for their entire length with walks between borders parallel with and following the lines of the enclosing walls.

## Contrasting colour schemes

In these walks there are flowers in plenty. There is a paeony walk, an iris border with a sunny aspect—irises like their rhizomes to be well baked in the summer—and there are lupins. Below the west wall nearer the lower end of the garden there is a herbaceous walk, its borders filled with soft pink and mauve, grey, blue and white flowers. In direct contrast to the soft colours of this border, flower borders on the southern side of the garden are planted in a carefully arranged scheme in strong colours. Delphiniums in shades of blue and purple, yellow and orange heliopsis, erigerons, scarlet poppies, the old crimson *Monarda* Cambridge Scarlet, so effective with purple salvias, and many others make a feast of rich colours in full view from the upper terrace. To lessen work, this border, which extends for the length of the garden, is planted partly with flowering shrubs. The transition from herbaceous plants to shrubs is gradual; groups of perennials being planted amongst the shrubs, and certain shrubs, chosen for the decorative effect of their foliage, and others because they flower during summer, amongst the herbaceous plants.

At Falkland, groups of cherry, philadelphus, weigela, ceanothus, cytisus and many other trees and shrubs give height and substance to the planting bordering the central glade. The contrast between the curving lines of the glade and the straight lines of the iris, peony and other walks adds to the interest and variety of the gardens to which several specimen trees, casting their shadows on the lawn, impart a feeling of maturity.

Interest should be reawakened at or near the limits of gardens and at Falkland there is a formal rose garden with a lily pool and fountain in the centre, its colours vivid against the dark green of the enclosing yew hedges and grey stone wall of outbuildings. This garden is, by its formality and the colours of the roses, a pleasing contrast to the prevailing summer greens of the glade leading to it.

Attached to the stables is the Royal Tennis Court, built by King James V in 1539. This tennis court or 'catch-spiel' is of special interest, as it is the only real-tennis court in Scotland to survive from the Stuart period. The only other one of comparable age or interest is at Hampton Court. The game was originally played by hand, racquets not being in universal use when the court was built—and it was not until the next century that a net was introduced to replace a fringed or tasselled rope. In 1628 'new pavement' was brought to be laid out in the court. Here the Stuart kings and their courtiers played what is one of the oldest and most difficult of ball games. Some of their tennis balls are now to be seen in the palace.

## AN ILLUSION OF DISTANCE
*Plates 63, 64*

As they were, the gardens at Lower Sandhill, Halland, in Sussex, consisted of a rose garden, a tennis court and a small croquet lawn. There was no principal way round them and it was necessary to make gardens suitable to the character of the house. To do this the lawn to the west of the drive as one enters from the road was extended along the northern side and round the western end of the tennis court to lead into a walk which, in turn, brings one back to the terrace on the south front. Flanked by curving borders of trees and shrubs in which cherries and laburnums overhang stretches of azaleas, berberis and lilies, the winding glade is lovely and interesting all the year round.

Character is given to the long walk by cypresses which, planted formally in pairs, extend for its entire length. This repetition of the same kind of trees at regular intervals makes for an apparent lengthening of the walk. Sheltered from the north by tall evergreen hedges, from it one can enjoy the prospect of horses and cattle grazing in and giving life to the park-like meadows. At its eastern end a little paved court under the shadow of the oast house with a seat standing back in its scented flower-filled beds gives a view down the length of the walk.

The oast house, a building so characteristic of this part of the country, rises like a circular tower. Formerly a separate building, it has been connected to the house by additions, a library and garden room, the latter giving access to a billiard room recently made in part of the oast house. In these additional buildings the roof lines, which are not always studied as they should be, have been carefully considered. The steeper roof of the barn rising higher than the low roofs of the sun room and library connect the barn with the main block of the house in a most attractive way.

*Converging angles*

To overcome the awkwardness created by converging angles a long low bank below the terrace was planted with *Juniperus chinensis pfitzeriana*, low berberis, *Cotoneaster horizontalis* and *Genista hispanica*. These shrubs have now covered the bank with the result that the difference in the angles is unnoticeable and, too, the thick mainly evergreen growths, in themselves so decorative, are practically impervious to weeds, a distinct advantage in these days of scarcity of help.

A straight drive leads from the road to the house and the question arose whether to make the drive separate from, or to let it run through the gardens. To separate the drive by hedges or trees and shrubs would have made the gardens private. To make it run through the gardens would create a more spacious and altogether finer effect. Lower Sandhill is in the country and it was not necessary to consider privacy too much. It was decided to make the drive a part of the gardens.

Lower Sandhill shows what can be done by adapting existing features to other than their original use. As an example, a swimming pool has been constructed in what was formerly a small farmyard. Dressing rooms have been built into the end of a barn, the centre part of which is a sunny shelter overlooking the pool. With its breast-high flint and brick walls, smoothly cut lawn and borders filled with lavender and lilies, roses covering the walls and clothing the heavy oak posts that support the barn roof, the swimming pool court has become a kind of social rendezvous in the gardens. Japanese maples, *Acer palmatum dissectum atropurpureum*, in square wooden tubs at the corners of the rectangular pool, add to the decorative effect.

## A SENSE OF OUTDOOR PROPORTION
### *Plates 65, 66*

At Llannerch Park, the house standing on ground levelled in its well timbered deer park, commands extensive views over the gardens, the park and on to the river flowing in the valley beneath. It is an extensive and lovely panorama. The scenery is fine and the site was in all probability chosen so that it should be overlooked from the principal windows of the house.

The gardens were of necessity terraced and from the highest terrace a flight of steps some 60 feet long and wide in proportion, descends to a second terrace. This second terrace was made into a long, formal, paved flower garden. From it a second flight of steps also 60 feet in length, descends to yet another terrace, this a lawn.

There is a sense of outdoor proportion which should govern everything the garden designer does. This awareness of outdoor proportion is quite different from that used in designing a house and, I suppose, becomes keener with practice. As an instance, after I had completed another set of gardens a summer-house was built at the end of a long principal vista. The summer-house foreshortened the vista to a surprising extent. The owner asked what was wrong and how it could be made right. I suggested that the white-columned pavilion should be painted green, the nearest shade we could get to the surrounding turf and trees, and that two flowering cherries should be planted to overhang it. Painted green and shaded by cherries, the pavilion was much less noticeable.

## Architectural values enhanced by trees

Nowhere is good architecture seen to greater advantage than when it is, as it were, supported by mature trees. On the upper terrace at Llannerch Park there are to the west the cloisters, which were built as part of the garden scheme and which, turning at right angles, lead into a loggia. Elms and beeches growing tall behind them, furnish a green background which enhances the effect of the Italianate cloisters and loggia immensely. From the loggia looking centrally down the length of the garden there are the pool and the long canal; it is a paved garden, with plants spreading luxuriantly on to the flagstones, and filling the borders with colour. With the reflections in the water the garden is opulent with colour and to the left, in the valley, there is the river, a silvery stream in the distance. This garden is planted to give a succession of colour until late in the year.

A villa on the French Riviera (see page 82)

# 7

# *Garden Plans*

## A LAKELAND GARDEN

The garden on this site had to be designed with a series of vantage points from which to appreciate the surroundings—the hills to the north and the placid, light-reflecting surface of Lake Windermere to the south. There had, of course, to be boundaries but these were made as unnoticeable as possible, for instance in places the boundary was a ha-ha (A), invisible, so that the turf of the meadow seemed only an extension of the lawn in the garden.

Also because of the nature of the landscape simplicity was necessarily one of the keynotes. Terraces, sheltered, and as wide as the contours allowed, helped to overcome this problem, and it was important that in every part there were good proportions. Terraces were, too, the answer to the fact that on sloping ground some level parts are required.

Thus two terraces on the south front were made, the lower having flower borders (B)—almost the only flowers in the gardens other than shrubs—for this had to be a peaceful retreat in which the owners could be as indolent as they wished.

Below the terraces a meadow fell in an easy slope to a farmhouse, partly hidden in trees. To the left of the meadow in a long narrow stretch of ground (C), a part of the site, there were several oaks and these, with some Scots pines and a few Douglas firs, were sufficient to give the screening and shelter necessary. Levelling, mowing and rolling changed the turf into a lawn, and with the addition of some hardy rhododendrons, planted in front of the existing trees, the ground became a rhododendron glade (C). This can be seen from the windows and terraces, and its colours, vivid in their green setting, seem to extend the gardens considerably beyond their apparently natural boundaries.

To the north of the short drive a lawn (D) was sown. In its flanking borders there are more rhododendrons. A group of *Rosa moyesii*, its flowers blood-red behind the yellow *Hypericum patulum henryi*, and red and purple ericas and *Berberis thunbergii* echo the colours on the hills. The glade (E) sweeps round behind the buildings and returns to the terraces at their western end, a continuous walk varying all the way in the character of its planting.

In this country, gardens in spring and early summer are lovely with flowering trees and shrubs, but this opulence of colour and fragrance has to be paid for during the late summer by a comparative scarcity of flowering shrubs. However, to compensate there are roses and perennials. Many hybrid tea and floribunda roses bloom more or less continuously and if they are left to grow

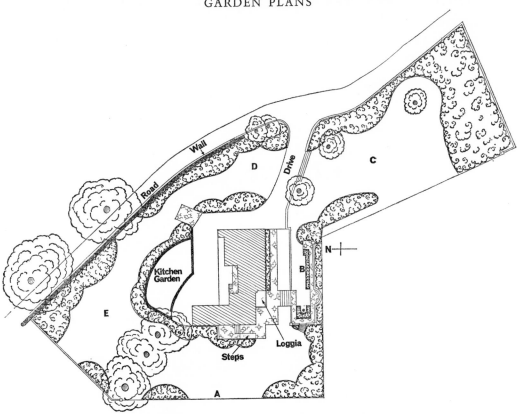

into fair-sized bushes they really become shrubs. If, however, you want them to grow in this way be content with thinning the growths well down into the bush instead of giving them the usual hard pruning. Although the separate flowers will be smaller some varieties would furnish a great deal of colour for a long time. They would really become what Nature intended them to be, almost perpetual-flowering shrubs. It is easy, however, to imagine the horror with which the trained gardener would view such a request.

In the glade there are several groups of Frensham and other floribunda roses, as well as a number of old-fashioned roses. The introduction of floribunda roses was a boon to gardeners for they, like old-fashioned and species roses, can be planted in glades without upsetting our sense of the fitness of gardening etiquette. And they give a lot of colour for a long time.

## A SMALL TOWN GARDEN

This small garden would be suitable for many town houses. The site is rectangular. A loggia opens on the south to an octagonal court and on the east to an open lawn with a stone sundial or bird bath standing in the semicircular curve. Paving, which defines the shape of the lawn, makes this into a formal flower garden.

On its northern boundary a paved walk goes between herbaceous borders (A) to a little rose garden at its far end. Here a fountain pool and figure give a note of interest. The rose garden is continued as a rose walk along the bottom of the garden and the fountain forms a focal point between the herbaceous walk and the rose walk.

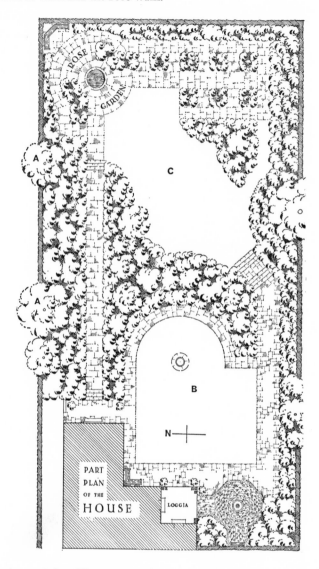

This garden consists mainly of four principal parts, the lawn (B) near the house, the herbaceous walk, the rose garden and the glade of flowering trees and shrubs (C) which crosses the garden diagonally and leads to the pool in the north-eastern corner. It is a pleasant change to walk from the glade into the more formal parts and the trees and shrubs which fill the borders give form and substance and make the garden interesting all the year round. In such a glade there can be the lovely foliage of Japanese maples, cherries, lilacs, azaleas and, if space allows, rhododendrons. By

planting a few trees of medium size—cherries and laburnums—the different parts can be separated in a pleasing way. For the sake of their substance and evergreen foliage some conifers should be included. *Chamaecyparis allumii, C. lawsoniana* or *C. fraseri* are all close-growing, an important consideration in a comparatively small space, and they remain furnished from the base upwards.

## A RECTANGULAR GARDEN

With straight boundaries, this is a plan for a small rectangular garden, the type that is more often than not with nothing to give it interest. Variety is said to be the spice of life, and to nothing can this apply more forcibly than to gardens. The garden is divided into three parts. The house opens to a lawn surrounded with flower borders and flagged walks. The second part is a rose garden, also with paved paths, the panel of rose beds arranged in a diamond pattern. The third is a quiet garden of lawn with a fountain and pool (A) as its chief interest. The first garden with its open lawn is the best preparation for the rose garden, filled with beds and colour. The third, which is entirely different from the first two, has a pool built against the wall with a fountain central on the long flagged walk which connects the three gardens. Instead of the more usual vista through the centre of the garden the wide walk on the western boundary continues through the first lawn and the rose garden to lead into the third garden. Another walk on the eastern side leads back to the terrace and the house.

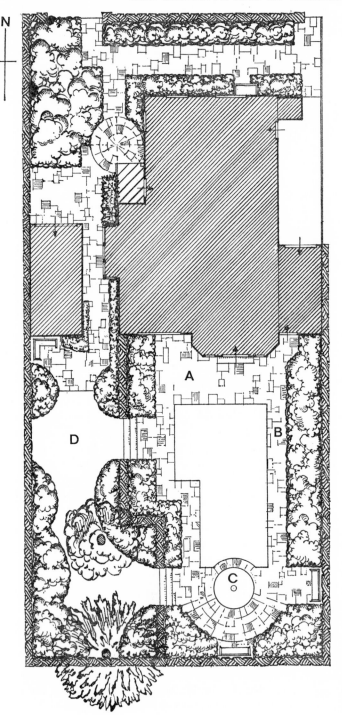

## A TINY GARDEN

The large window of the principal sitting room opens to a terrace and paving (A). A paved walk (B) from the terrace is continued against the flower border for the length of the garden. The pool with its central fountain figure (C) at the far end and on an axial line central with the bay window, makes an interesting focal point. The formal garden is separated by a yew hedge from the little glade (D) on its western side.

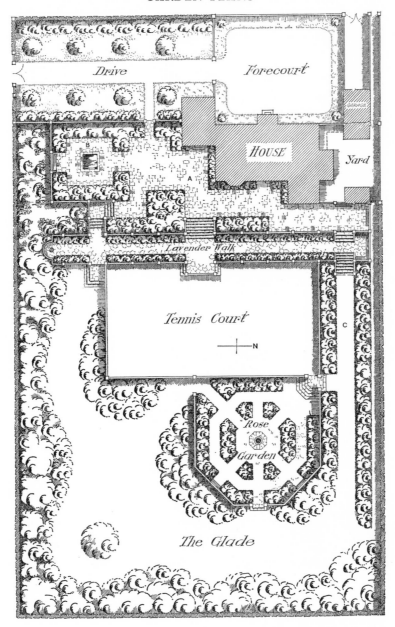

## ELABORATE TREATMENT OF A SMALL GARDEN

For its size this is a rather elaborate garden. The house opens on to a paved terrace (A) leading into a pool garden (B). The borders around the pool garden are planted to be full of colour for as long a time as possible. It is a garden on sloping ground and steps from the main terrace lead down to a lavender walk which extends for the width of the site. From here more steps go down to the tennis court and to the glade lawn. Below the tennis court a semi-octagonal rose garden, with its formal design and lovely colours, adds very much to the interest of the garden as a whole. The tennis court and the rose garden are enclosed by the curving glade, the borders of which are planted with flowering trees and shrubs, cherries, lilacs, laburnams, azaleas and rhododendrons. Along the northern boundary a herbaceous walk (C) leads back to the terrace.

The tennis court is approximately central in this garden and could be left as a lawn for croquet or other games. The glade follows the natural contours of the slopes and, by its contrast with the formal rose garden and herbaceous walk, makes a varied and interesting garden.

## A HERB GARDEN

The treatment for this garden is in keeping with the architectural character of the house. It is a lavender or herb garden with brick paving and enclosed by clipped yew or box hedges. Ceanothus and other taller growing shrubs are planted to fill the corners and there is an opening central on the doors leading into a rose garden. The lavender is an excellent preparation for the colours of the roses. Such a garden could be planted in various ways; it could be a herb garden or a white garden or indeed it could be kept to any colour scheme to suit individual taste.

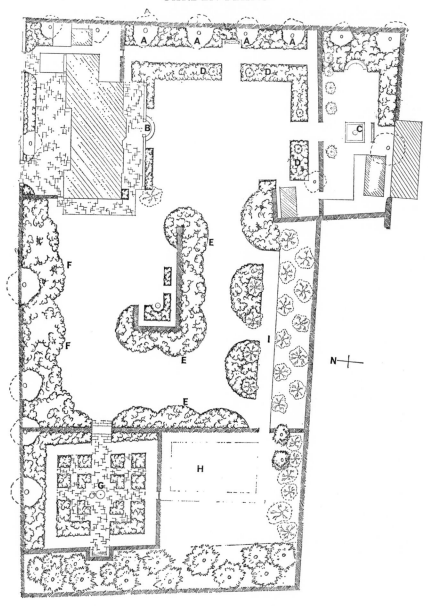

# A GARDEN ON CHALK

In this garden the site which slopes from the terrace to the south, is enclosed on the east by tall poplars (A) and other trees. There are trees, too, making a leafy background beyond the southern boundary.

Steps (B) lead from the terrace to the lawn and from the centre window there is a vista through to a pool (C) in a second garden. In this sunlit space beyond the opening in the hedge, a single jet rises like a silver spear, seemingly more light than water, to fall with a musical splash into the pool. The pool mirrors the lighted green of the trees in an almost mystical way, so charmingly do the shades dissolve into each other. But lovely as the various shades of green are, colour was needed and the beds on the eastern side (D) and borders to the south (D) are filled with flowering plants. In these borders there are tall delphiniums, satin pink sidalceas with next to them the silvery-pinks of *Salvia turkestanica*, *Monarda* Croftway Pink and *Artemisia lactiflora*, the tall cream plumes of which tone beautifully with almost any colour. The borders are enriched with several groups of purple *Salvia splendens*.

The alkaline soil made it impossible to use azaleas and ericaceous plants but the borders which form the glade going to the west (E) are filled with *Berberis thunbergii* and *B. wilsonae* and groups of species roses. *Cotinus coggygria foliis purpureis* likes the chalky soil and has grown into big bushes, in front of which scarlet and amber dahlias give splashes of vivid colour. On the northern boundary under the shade of overhanging trees (F) the long grass is planted with drifts of narcissi to flower in the spring and later there are colchicums.

There are enough rose species in this border to give it form and the long grass in itself forms a pattern with the mown turf of the lawn.

On the western side of the garden steps lead into a rose garden (G) enclosed by yew hedges, from which again a path leads into the kitchen garden (H) to return to a walk between fruit trees (I) on the southern side.

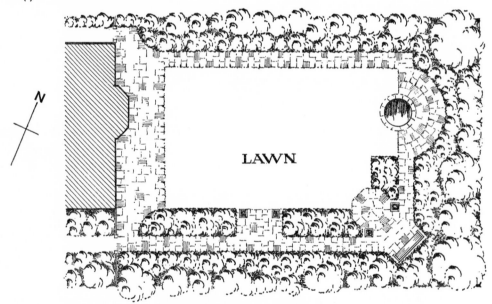

**LAWN**

## SIMPLE FORMALITY

This is a small formal flower garden with a fountain and pool in the semicircular recess opposite the bay window. The paved walk gives a dry way from the terrace to the seat on the south side. It is a simple but effective treatment for a limited space.

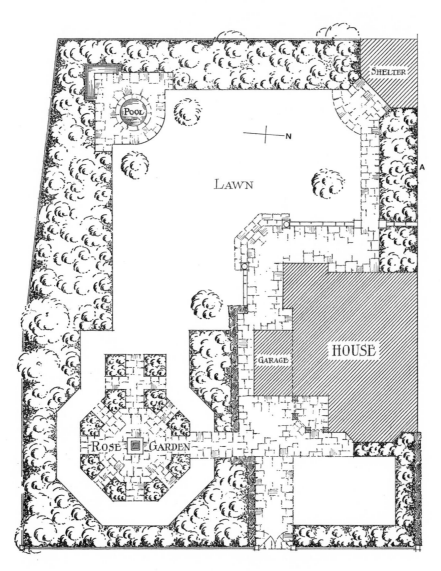

## EASY TO MAINTAIN

Because of its straightforward lines this small garden would be easy to maintain. The only herbaceous border (A) is the one from the house to the shelter in the far corner but the borders surrounding the lawn have, amongst the shrubs with which they are planted, groups of herbaceous plants. From the lawn one comes to the rose garden, in the centre of which stands a sundial on paving. In the south-west corner of the garden, diagonally opposite to the house, is a pool and seat, central on the steps leading from the terrace.

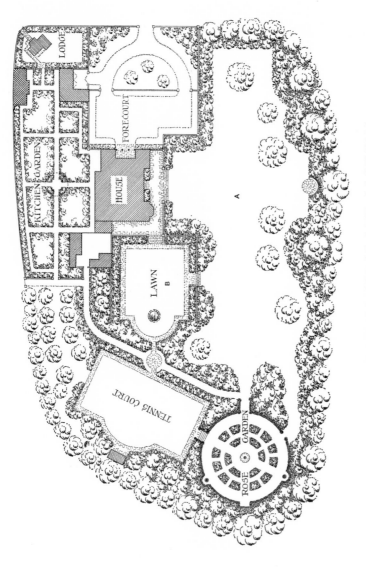

## CONNECTING SEPARATE GARDENS

A tennis court, a rose garden, a formal garden, a fairly extensive glade and a kitchen garden are the main points of interest in this garden. The house opens on to a paved terrace on two fronts and from this terrace wide steps lead down to the glade lawn (A) and a second flight to the formal garden (B). The space between the tennis court and the kitchen garden is planted with fruit trees which, with narcissi, the paler varieties, such as Mrs E. H. Krelage, in the turf beneath them, make a charming setting for the tennis court on this side. The flowering trees and shrubs which fill the borders in the glade give substance to the gardens and separate the different parts.

Yew hedges backed by flowering cherries and other trees make the rose garden a separate feature and, with the shrubs of the glade, give the interest of gardens separate yet connected by the various walks.

## AN OCTAGONAL GARDEN

A paved path (A) leads from the gate to the front door, with a side entrance into the garden. A wide terrace (B) extends round the western and southern fronts of the house, from which steps lead down to a formal pool garden. The octagonal shape of the garden is accentuated by a continuous border of flagstones. To the east from this garden there is a long herbaceous walk, to the right of which at the end is a rose garden (C). This rose garden is of unusual design and it leads to a long glade (D). This, planted chiefly with flowering trees and shrubs and extending from the rose garden to steps leading to the terrace, is generously wide and its northern end leads through a wrought iron gate to the forecourt.

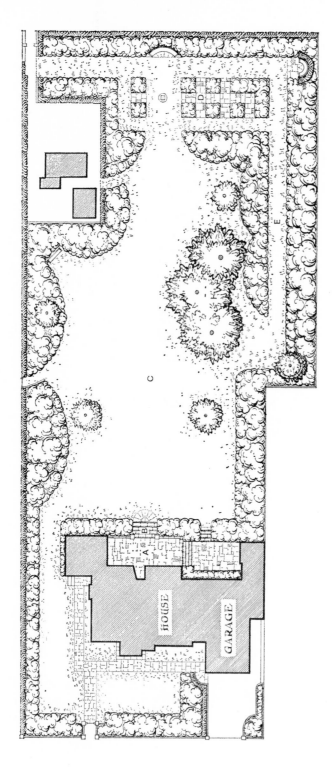

## AN ILLUSION OF SPACE

The curving lines of the glade which extends to the rose walk at the far end, make the garden appear larger than would otherwise be the case. The house opens on to a terrace (A) from which steps (B) lead down to the lawn (C). Interest is awakened at the far end by the rose walk (D) which in turn leads into a herbaceous walk (E) and then back to the main lawn near the house.

Originally there was a rose garden in the lawn just below the terrace and it can be seen how this made the whole garden appear so much smaller than it was. The three trees grouped together on the lawn, which dominate the garden in a very attractive way, are willows, but these trees grow quickly and every few years it is necessary to cut them back. Their strong new pendulous growths, however, furnish them again even the first year after cutting. Their soft green unfolding foliage is lovely in spring and, too, they separate the herbaceous walk from the main lawn.

# A SUBURBAN GARDEN

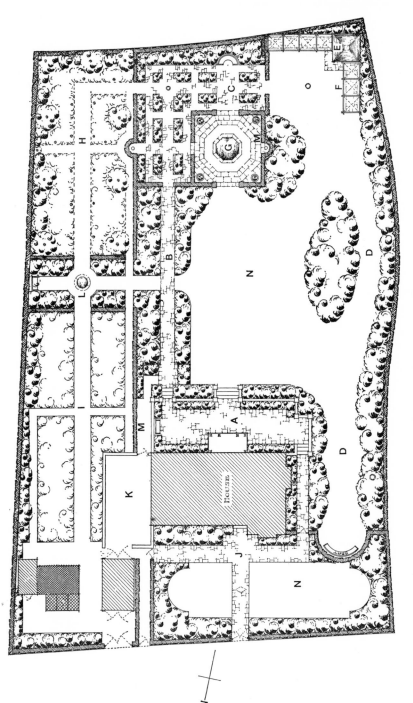

From the terrace (A) a paved or turf walk (B) leads between the flower-filled borders to a rose walk (C) which turns into the end of a glade lawn (D). Here, a shelter (E) built between two lengths of a pergola (F), gives a vista into the rose walk, another vista through curving borders of flowering shrubs and a third on to the centre lawn. Vines, clematis and climbing roses clothe the pergola with their foliage and flowers. The handsome leaves of *Vitis coignetiae* turn to a rich shade of claret before falling and purple clematis are lovely with the shell pink rose Albertine and the scarlet blooms of the climb-ing form of Ena Harkness.

In the right angle formed by the two sides of the rose garden a small paved court with a pool and fountain figure (G) give point to a charming vista from the principal garden door. Crossing the lawn there are curving borders of flower-ing shrubs and the centre path of the rose garden leads into the orchard (H) and turns into the kitchen garden (I). Other features are: (J) the paved forecourt; (K) the kitchen courtyard; (L) the dipping well; (M) the yew hedge, and (N) the lawn.

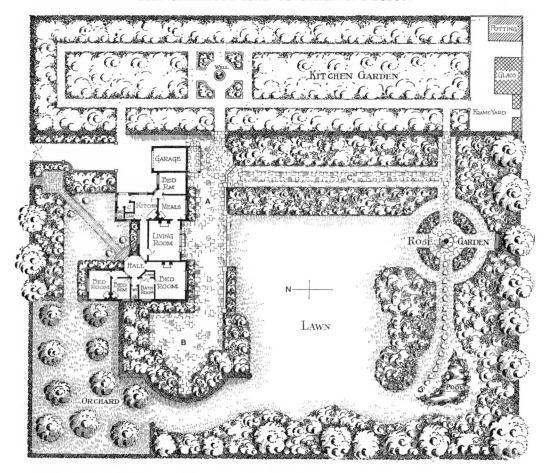

## A BUNGALOW GARDEN

The entrance from the road is cleverly concealed by hedges enclosing a square of paving, from which a path running diagonally through the lawn, leads to the front door. Doors from the living room lead on to the terrace and a wide opening at the far end of the lawn gives a view of the rose garden.

On the west the terrace (A) extends into a semicircular formal garden (B). This garden is enclosed by a yew hedge behind which a walk leads from the orchard into the principal lawn. There is a little pool and rock garden in the south-west corner, to which Japanese azaleas, Japanese maples, some of the lovely *Iris kaempferi* and low-growing junipers give a slightly Japanese character.

The rose garden has only four beds but, to include a greater number of varieties, roses are planted in the outer borders. From here the walk continues into the kitchen garden but a paved walk (C) turning at right angles leads back to the terrace at its eastern end.

In this garden the wide steps in front of the living room create an illusion of space and from the terrace and the windows borders filled with colour would be visible the greater part of the year.

The terrace is continued into the kitchen garden to a well-head set in four beds. The beds are filled with floribunda roses with an edging of nepeta. This is an obliging plant, the flowers of which take on an unexpected depth of colour when there is enough of it.

This treatment carries the feeling of the terrace and pleasure garden into the kitchen garden which is in itself attractive.

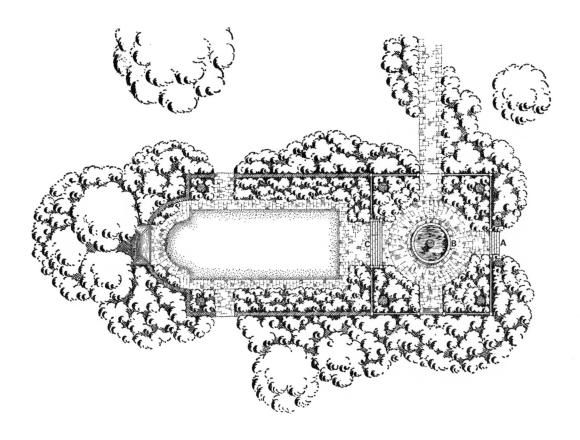

## A FORMAL GARDEN

Steps (A) lead down into a paved pool garden (B) from which again wide steps (C) lead into a formal flower garden with a pavilion at the far end. The formal design of this garden is increased by the flagged walk between the borders and the central panel of the lawn. These gardens are surrounded with trees and shrubs which increase their sunken feeling. The pool and flower garden would be complete in themselves or equally well they could form part of a larger garden.

## A FEELING OF SPACIOUSNESS

The curving borders enclosing the main lawn give a feeling of comparative spaciousness. Nothing is finer in English gardens than trees standing in lawn and in this lawn there are several crataegus and prunus. The colours of flowering cherries and Mollis and Ghent azaleas, other than azaleas with strong orange flowers, go beautifully together. Any garden seems more attractive if one can walk round it without retracing one's steps and in this garden, from the formal flower garden (A) to the west of the house, there is a wide straight way (B) between the cherries and azaleas leading into the rose garden, and then back to the main lawn.

A note of emphasis and contrast with the azaleas, berberis and other lower growing shrubs is given by the four conifers at the lower end of the garden.

# Index

(Abbreviation: d = line drawing or plan)

*Abelia chinensis*, 28
*Acer* Osakazuki, 60
   *palmatum dissectum atropurpurem*, 60
*Acorus gramineus pusillus*, 43
Alder, 46
*Alisma plantago-aquatica*, 44
Alnus (alder), 46
Althaea (hollyhock), 26–7
*Aquilegia glandulosa*, 43
Ardleigh, Chigwell, 67, Pl. 25
*Artemisia arborescens*, 28
*Aruncus sylvester*, 43
Ascot, Berkshire: Boden's Ride, Pl. 12
Aspen, 46
Aster, 25
Astilbe, 43
Aviary, The, Southall, 65–6
  glade, Pl. 24
  lake, Pl. 23
Azalea dell: Dartington Hall, 54

Banks, waterside: plants for, 42–4
Bedfordshire: Westfields, 89–91, Pls. 8, 15, 16, 19,
    51, 52
  Woburn Abbey, 22–4, 24d
Beech, 49
*Berberis*, 54
  Comet, 51
  *darwinii*, 52
  *linearifolia* Orange King, 52
  *rubrostilla*, 81
  *stenophylla*, 51
  *thunbergii*, 50, 51, 81
    *atropurpurea*, 81
  *verruculosa*, 52, 81
  *wilsonae*, 51

Berkshire: Ascot: Boden's Ride, Pl. 12
*Betula pendula* (silver birch):
  temporary planting, 21
Birch, silver: temporary planting, 21
Blue: borders of, 26
Boden's Ride, Ascot: pergola, Pl. 12
Bog garden: plants for, 43–4
Border, herbaceous, 25–31, 29d
  Bowhill, Pl. 6
  Hascombe Court, Pl. 47
  Langham Hall, Pl. 39
Boundaries: definition of, 11–12
Bowhill, Chichester: herbaceous borders, Pl. 6
Bramble, *see Rubus*
Buckinghamshire: Marlow: Old Parsonage, Pl. 17
*Buddleia alternifolia*, 28, 57
Bungalow garden, 116d
Busbridge Wood, Godalming: rhododendron glade,
  Pl. 18
  rose garden, Pl. 7
*Butomus umbellatus*, 43

Californian tree poppy, *see Romneya coulteri*
*Calluna vulgaris hammondii*, 62
Camellia, 57
*Caltha palustris*, 43
'Catch-spiel', 98
*Ceratostigma willmottianum*, 28
Chalk: garden on, 109–10, 109d
*Chamaecyparis lawsoniana*, 49
  *allumii*, 13, 14, 49, Pl. 59
  *fletcheri*, 14
Cherry, *see Prunus*
Chestham Park, Sussex, 93–5, Pls. 59, 60
  glade, Pl. 58
Chichester: Bowhill, Pl. 6
Chigwell, Essex: Ardleigh, 67, Pl. 25

*Choisya ternata*, 27, 28
*Cistus corbariensis*, 28
  *cyprius*, 28
  *loretii*, 28
  *purpureus*, 28
  Silver Pink, 28
Climate: influence, 13
Colchester, Essex: Langham Hall, 76–8, Pl. 39
Colours: seen from distance, 45
  used on terraces, 67
Colour schemes, 29d, 30–1
  in glades, 50–1
Contrast of design, 12
  between separate gardens within main garden, 14–15, 18, 21, 22d, 22–4
  connecting contrasting gardens, 112d
*Cornus alba* Westonbirt, 46
*Cotinus coggygria foliis purpureis*, 57–8
*Cotoneaster*, 52–3
  *bullatus*, 53
  *franchetii*, 26, 52
  *frigidus*, 52, 53
    *vicari*, 52
  *henryanus*, 53
  *horizontalis*, 52
  *hupehensis*, 53
  *lacteus*, 53
  *rotundifolius* (*C. hookeri*), 53
  *salicifolius*, 53
Cottage, The, Le Touquet, 68–9, Pl. 28
Courtyard, 15–17
  French Riviera, Pl. 48
  Hoare's Bank, Fleet Street, Pl. 3
  in Italy, 15
  Pilgrim's Cottage, Pl. 46
  plants for, 17
  Stockholm, 16d
  White House, Highgate, Pl. 4
*Crataegus monogyna* (quickthorn), 12
Crocus, 55
*Cupressocyparis leylandii*, 49
*Cypripedium reginae*, 43
*Cytisus battandieri*, 28, 57

Dartington Hall, Devon, 91–2
  azalea dell, Pl. 54
  glade, lawn and stairway, Pl. 53
  view from, Pl. 55
Delphinium, 26

Denbighshire: Llannerch Park, 100–1, Pls. 65, 66
*Deutzia* Contrast, 56
  *longifolia veitchii*, 56
  Magician, 56
  *rosea*, 56
    *campanulata*, 56
Devon: Dartington Hall, 91–2, Pls. 53, 54, 55
Distance, illusions of, 12

Edging plants: for rose gardens, 35–6
*Erica arborea alpina*, 56
*Escallonia iveyi*, 27
Essex: Chigwell: Ardleigh, 67, Pl. 25
  Colchester: Langham Hall, 76–8, Pl. 39
  Frinton-on-Sea: Old Hall Cottage, 67–8, Pl. 27
  Woodford, 69, Pls. 29, 30
*Euonymus alatus*, 58
  *europaeus*, 58
  *yedoensis*, 58

Fagus (beech), 49
Falkland Palace, Fife, 97–9, Pl. 62
Fife: Falkland Palace, 97–9, Pl. 62
Fittleworth, Sussex: Mill House, 80, Pls. 43, 44
Fleet Street: Hoare's Bank, Pl. 3
Fontainebleau, 12
Formal design, 13–14, 117d
  contrasting with informal, 22–4
Forsythia, 50–1
*Fothergilla major*, 54
  *monticola*, 54
Four Oaks, Warwickshire: Hillside, 74–6, Pls. 11, 37, 38
France: Fontainebleau, 12
  Le Touquet, The Cottage, 68–9, Pl. 28
  Paris: Louvre, 12
  Rambouillet, 12
  Riviera villa, 82, Pl. 48
  Saint Cloud, 12
  Versailles, 12
French gardens, 12
Frinton-on-Sea, Essex: Old Hall Cottage, 67–8, Pl. 27
Frognal, London, 66, Pl. 26

Garden glade, 48
  Chestham Park, Pl. 58
  Old Parsonage, Pl. 17
  Westfields, Pl. 19

*Genista aetnensis*, 58
*Gentiana asclepiadea*, 43
Glades, 19, 48–58, Pl. 20
    Aviary, The, Pl. 24
    background planting, 49
    Busbridge Wood, Pl. 18
    Chestham Park, Pl. 58
    colour schemes, 50–1
    Dartington Hall, Pl. 53
    Hungerdown House, Pl. 34
    interest through year, 49–50
    Old Parsonage, Pl. 17
    planning, 53–4
    types, 48–9
    Westfields, Pl. 19
Godalming, Surrey: Busbridge Wood, Pls. 7, 18
Green: aesthetic value of, 14–15
Grey foliage plants, 70
Gunnera, 47

*Halesia carolina*, 46
*Halimium ocymoides*, 28
Halland, Sussex: Lower Sandhill, 99–100, Pls. 63, 64
Hamamelis, 54
Hascombe Court, Surrey, 44, 82–6
    formal paved garden, Pl. 13
    herbaceous borders, Pl. 47
    terrace, Pls. 5, 49
*Hebe* Autumn Glory, 30
    *traversii*, 30
Hedges: for boundaries, 12, 49
    effect in design, 15
Height: emphasising, 17
*Heliopsis patula*, 31
Herbaceous border, 25–31, 29d
    Bowhill, Pl. 6
    Hascombe Court, Pl. 47
    Langham Hall, Pl. 39
    The Vern, Pl. 42
Herb garden, 108d
Herefordshire: The Vern, 79, Pl. 42
Heuchera, 36
Hibiscus, 28
Highgate: White House, 15–16, Pl. 4
Hillside, Four Oaks, Warwickshire, 74–6
    pool garden, Pl. 37
    rose garden, Pl. 11
    terrace and lawn, Pl. 38
Hilly gardens: advantages of, 19

Hoare's Bank, Fleet Street, Pl. 3
Holly, 12
Hollyhock, 26–7
*Holodiscus discolor ariaefolius*, 30, 56
Hosta, 27, 43
Hungerdown House, Wiltshire, 21, 71–4
    formal garden, Pl. 36
    glade, Pl. 34
    house and terrace, Pl. 35
    lily pool, Pl. 33
    plan, 20d
Hydrangea, 58, 68
*Hypericum moserianum*, 28
    *patulum forrestii*, 28
    Rowallane, 28

Ilex (holly), 12
Illusions: of distance, 12
    of space, in small garden, 114d
Informal gardens: contrasting with formal, 22–4
*Iris*, 70, 98
    borders of, 26
    *kaempferi*, 43
    *laevigata*, 43
    planting, 26
    *sibirica*, 43
Italian gardens, 12
Italy: courtyards in, 15
Itchenor: Pilgrim's Cottage, 80–1, Pls. 45, 46

Japan: Kyoto: Katsura Villa, Pl. 22
    Kyoto: Tenryuji Temple, Pl. 21
Japanese gardens, 59–64
    ornaments in, 63
    plan, imaginary, 62–3
    planning, 60
    plants for, 60–2
    symbolism in design, 59–60
    types, 59–60
Jedburgh: Monteviot, 92–3, Pls. 9, 56, 57
*Juniperus chinensis*, 13, 61
    *aurea*, 13–14
    *pfitzeriana*, 60, 61
        pruning, 74
    *sabina tamariscifolia*, 60
    *virginiana*, 61

Katsura Villa, Kyoto, Pl. 22

Kent: Knole, Pl. 1
  Penshurst, Pl. 2
  Sandwich: White House, 69–70, Pls. 31, 32
Knole, Kent, Pl. 1
Kyoto: Katsura Villa, Pl. 22
  Tenryuji Temple, Pl. 21

Laburnum, 51, 54
  *vossii*, 54
Lake: garden made beside, 102–3, 103d
  as principal feature, 65–6
  Southall: The Aviary, Pl. 23
Langham Hall, Colchester, 76–8
  herbaceous walk, Pl. 39
Large gardens, 19–21
Lawn: contrasting with flower garden, 14–15
Level gardens: advantages of, 19
*Ligularia clivorum*, 47
Lilac, *see* Syringa
*Lilium candidum*, 27
  *regale*, 27, 62
  setting for, 62
  *tigrinum*, 62
  *umbellatum*, 62
Lily, *see Lilium*
Llannerch Park, 100–1
  cloisters and pool, Pl. 65
  terrace and canal, Pl. 66
*Lobelia cardinalis* Queen Victoria, 43
London: Fleet Street, Hoare's Bank, Pl. 3
  Frognal, 66, Pl. 26
  Highgate, White House, 15–16, Pl. 4
Louvre, Paris, 12
Lower Sandhill, Sussex, 99–100, Pl. 63
  terrace, Pl. 64
*Lysimachia punctata*, 43

*Magnolia*, 55
  *grandiflora*, 55–6
Maple, *see Acer*
Marlow, Buckinghamshire: Old Parsonage, Pl. 17
Marshy ground: plants for, 43
Medium-sized gardens, 18–19
*Mertensia virginica*, 43
Michaelmas daisy, *see* Aster
Middlesex: Highgate: White House, 15–16, Pl. 4
  Southall: The Aviary, 65–6, Pls. 23, 24
Milles, Carl, 16
Mill House, Fittleworth, 80, Pl. 43

lawn walk and terrace, Pl. 44
Milton, Peterborough, 96–7, Pl. 61
Mimulus, 43
Moisture-loving plants, 43–4, 46–7
*Monarda didyma* Cambridge Scarlet, 43
Monteviot, Jedburgh, 92–3, Pls. 9, 57
  river garden, Pl. 56
Myrobalan plum, 49

Northamptonshire: Peterborough: Milton, 96–7, Pl. 61

Oakley, Bedfordshire: Westfields, 89–91, Pls. 8, 15, 16, 19, 51, 52
Octagonal garden, 113d
*Olearia haastii*, 30
  *macrodonta*, 30
Old Hall Cottage, Frinton-on-Sea, 67–8, Pl. 27
Old Parsonage, Marlow: glade, Pl. 17
*Omphalodes cappadocica*, 43
Ornaments: in Japanese garden, 63

*Paeonia*, 25
  *delavayi*, 54
  *lemoinei* Alice Harding, 54
    Souvenir de Maxime Cornu, 54
  *lutea*, 54
  *suffruticosa*, 54
  tree, 54
Paeony, *see Paeonia*
Paris: Louvre, 12
*Parrotia persica*, 54
Penshurst, Kent, Pl. 2
Perennials: moisture-loving, 43–4, 46–7
Pergola, 36
  Boden's Ride, Pl. 12
Perovskia, 30
Peterborough, Northamptonshire: Milton, 96–7, Pl. 61
*Philadelphus*, 27, 57
  Beauclerk, 57
  Belle Etoile, 57
  *coronarius*, 57
  *grandiflorus*, 67
*Phlomis fruticosa*, 28, 30, 31, 70
Phlox, 27, 43
Pilgrim's Cottage, Itchenor, 80–1, Pl. 45
  courtyard, Pl. 46
*Pinus mugo*, 61, 81

# INDEX

Plans, 102–18
Pool: altering, 44
  construction, 42
  position, 18
Poplar, *see Populus*
*Populus alba*, 46
  *nigra*, 46
  *tremula* (aspen), 46
*Potentilla*, 30, 58
  *fruticosa vilmoriniana*, 58
*Primula bulleyana*, 43
  *helodoxa*, 43
  *japonica*, 43
  *pulverulenta*, 43
  *sikkimensis*, 43
*Prunus amygdalo-persica pollardii*, 51
  avenue of, 55
  *avium flore pleno*, 54
  *cerasifera* (myrobalan plum), 49
  *hillieri* Spire, 54
  Hokusai, 55
  Kanzan, 55
  *padus watereri*, 55
  *sargentii*, 55, 93
  *serrulata rosea*, 55
  *subhirtella autumnalis*, 55
  Tai-Haku, 55
  Ukon, 55
  under-planting, 55
  *yedoensis*, 55
*Pyracantha*, 56
  *angustifolia*, 56
  *atalantioides*, 56
  *coccinea lalandii*, 56
  *rogersiana flava*, 56

Quickthorn, 12

Rambouillet, 12
Rectangular garden, 103–5, 104d, 105d, 106d
Repton, Humphry, 22, 96
*Rheum palmatum*, 47
Rhododendron, 45, 51, 56–7
  glade of, Pl. 18
  *nobleanum*, 56
  under-planting, 84
Ridge End, Worcestershire: rose garden, Pl. 10
Riviera, French: villa garden, 82, Pl. 48
Rock: in water garden, 42

Rock garden, 63–4
*Rodgersia pinnata*, 47
*Romneya coulteri*, 27, 30, 58
*Rosa* Albertine, 40
  Allgold, 27, 39
  Baccara, 38
  Belle Blonde, 38
  Cardinal de Richelieu, 79
  Champs Elysées, 38
  Charles de Mills, 79
  Christian Dior, 38
  climbing: selection, 40
  Climbing Alfred Carrière, 40
  Climbing Ena Harkness, 40
  Climbing Lady Hillingdon, 40
  Climbing Mme Abel Chatenay, 40
  Climbing Shot Silk, 40
  Climbing Spek's Yellow, 40
  Dame Edith Helen, 38
  Dr Van Fleet, 40
  Donald Prior, 39
  Else's Rival, 39
  Ena Harkness, 38
  Fantin Latour, 79
  Fashion, 39
  floribunda, 28, 37
    selection, 39
  Frühlingsgold, 61–2
  Gloire de Dijon, 40
  Gloire de France, 79
  Golden Fleece, 39
  Grace de Monaco, 38
  *hugonis*, 61
  hybrid teas: selection, 38–9
  Iceberg, 39
  Innocence, 38
  Irene of Denmark, 39
  Irish, 36
  Ivory Fashion, 39
  Lemon Pillar, 40
  Lilli Marlene, 39
  McCredy's Ivory, 38
  McCredy's Yellow, 38
  Madame Louise Laperrière, 38
  Marcia Stanhope, 38
  Mojave, 39
  Moulin Rouge, 39
  Orangeade, 39
  Orange Sensation, 39

*Rosa*—cont.
  Papa Meilland, 38
  Paul's Scarlet, 40
  Peace, 38
  Picture, 38
  Pink Favourite, 38
  Poulsen's Yellow, 27
  Prima Ballerina, 38
  qualities, 33
  ramblers: selection, 40
  Royalist, 38
  *rubrifolia*, 46, 79
  Silver Lining, 39
  Soraya, 39
  Sun Valley, 38
  Super Star, 39
  Sutter's Gold, 38
  Talisman, 39
  Tzigane, 39
  Virgo, 38
Rose, *see Rosa*
Rose gardens, 32–40, 33d, 34d, 35d, 37d
  Busbridge Wood, Pl. 7
  design, 32
  edging plants for, 35–6
  Hillside, Pl. 11
  Monteviot, Pl. 9
  Ridge End, Pl. 10
  Westfields, Pl. 8
*Rosmarinus* (rosemary), 30
Rotunda, Pls. 40, 41
Rowan, 46
Roxburgh: Jedburgh: Monteviot, 92–3, Pls. 9, 56, 57
*Rubus cockburnianus*, 46
Russian sage, *see Perovskia*

Sage, Russian, *see Perovskia*
*Sagittaria latifolia*, 44
Saint Cloud, 12
*Salix alba tristis*, 45
  *babylonica*, 45, 65
  *caprea*, 46
  *daphnoides*, 46
  *vitellina*, 45
    *britzensis*, 45
Sandwich, Kent: White House, 69–70, Pls. 31, 32
*Santolina chamaecyparissus*, 30
Seaside gardens, 67–70
*Senecio laxifolius*, 27–8, 70

Shrubs: borders of, 19
  form, beauty of, 51–2
  form, for Japanese gardens, 62
  in herbaceous border, 27–30, 29d
  for Japanese gardens, 60–2
  planting preparations, 50
  for poor soil, 50
  summer flowering, 57–8
  white-flowered, 27
Small gardens, 17–18, 103–5, 104d, 105d, 106d
  easy to maintain, 111d
  elaborate treatment, 107d, 107–8
  formal treatment, 110d
  illusion of space in, 114d
Snowdrop tree, *see Halesia*
Soil, poor: shrubs for, 50
*Sorbaria aitchisonii*, 46
*Sorbus aucuparia* (rowan), 46
Southall, Middlesex: The Aviary, 65–6, Pls. 23, 24
Space: creating illusion of, in small garden, 114d
*Spartium junceum*, 28, 57
*Spiraea*, 43, 46
  *arguta*, 56
  *ariaefolius* (*Holodiscus discolor ariaefolius*), 30, 56
  *prunifolia flore pleno*, 56
Stockholm: courtyard of garden, 16
Stonely Woods, Yorkshire, 78–9
  rotunda, Pls. 40, 41
  terrace garden, Pl. 41
Streams: construction, 42
  Westfields, Pl. 15
Suburban garden, 115d
  Godalming: Busbridge Wood, Pls. 7, 18
  Hascombe Court, 44, 82–6, Pls. 5, 13, 47, 49
  Windlesham: Westwoods, 44, 86–9, Pls. 14, 50
Sussex: Chestham Park, 93–5, Pls. 58, 59, 60
  Chichester: Bowhill, Pl. 6
  Fittleworth: Mill House, 80, Pls. 43, 44
  Halland: Lower Sandhill, 99–100, Pls. 63, 64
  Itchenor: Pilgrim's Cottage, 80–1, Pls. 45, 46
Sweden: Stockholm, 16
Symbolism in Japanese gardens, 59–60
Symmetry, 14
*Syringa*, 51

*Taxodium distichum*, 46
*Taxus baccata fastigiata aurea*, 14
  *standishii*, 14
Tennis court: sixteenth-century, 98

# INDEX

Tenryuji Temple, Kyoto, Pl. 21
Terrace, 12
    colour on, 67
*Thalictrum glaucum*, 31
*Thuja lobii*, 49
Touquet, Le: The Cottage, 68–9, Pl. 28
Town garden, small, 103–5, 104d
Trees: borders of, 19
    form, for Japanese gardens, 62
    planting preparations, 50
    for symmetrical planting, 14
    temporary planting, 21
    for waterside, 45–6
Trillium, 43
Trollius, 43
Tulipa, 55
Turf: importance of, 13
*Typha angustifolia*, 44

Vern, The, Herefordshire, 79, Pl. 42
Veronica, shrubby, *see Hebe*
Versailles, 12
*Viburnum burkwoodii*, 56
    *carlesii*, 56
    *opulus*, 46
        *sterile*, 46
    *tinus*, 56
    *tomentosum plicatum*, 46
Viola: in rose gardens, 35–6
Vistas, 44–5

Walls, dry: plants for, 36
Warwickshire: Four Oaks: Hillside, 74–6, Pls. 11, 37, 38
Water gardens, 41–7
    construction, 42
    formal, 47, 90–1

informal, 89–90
    plants for, 42–4, 46–7
    rock, use in, 42
    trees for, 45–6
    Westfields, Pls. 15, 16, 52
    Westwoods, Pl. 14
Weigela, 56
Well-head, Pl. 36
    use, 18
Westfields, Bedfordshire, 89–91
    glade, Pl. 19
    pools and canal, Pl. 51
    rose garden and lily pool, Pl. 8
    stream, Pl. 15
    water garden, Pls. 16, 52
Westwoods, Surrey, 44, 86–9, Pl. 50
    pool, Pl. 14
White: borders of, 27
White House, Highgate, 15–16, Pl. 4
White House, Sandwich Bay, 69–70, Pl. 32
    lily pool, Pl. 31
Willow, *see Salix*
Wiltshire: Hungerdown House, 20d, 21, 71–4, Pls. 33, 34, 35, 36
Windermere, Lake: garden beside, 102–3, 103d
Windlesham, Surrey: Westwoods, 44, 86–9, Pls. 14, 50
Wisteria, 55
Woburn Abbey, 22–4
    formal gardens, 24d
Woodford, 69, Pls. 29, 30
Woodland glade, 48, Pl. 20
Worcestershire: Ridge End, Pl. 10

Yellow: borders of, 26–7
Yew, *see Taxus*
Yorkshire: Stonely Woods, 78–9, Pls. 40, 41